Britain's Most Depraved Killers

First published in 2014

A catalogue record for this book is available from the British Library

ISBN: 978-0-85733-718-4

Published by Haynes Publishing, Sparkford, Yeovil,
Somerset BA22 7JJ, UK
Tel: 01963 442030 Fax: 01963 440001
Int. tel: +44 1963 442030 Int. fax: +44 1963 440001
E-mail: sales@haynes.co.uk
Website: www.haynes.co.uk

Haynes North America Inc., 861 Lawrence Drive, Newbury Park, California 91320, USA

Images © Mirrorpix

Creative Director: Kevin Gardner
Designed for Haynes by BrainWave

Printed and bound in the US

Britain's Most Depraved Killers

From The Case Files of

SUNDAY PEOPLE and Mirror

Claire Welch

Contents

Introduction	1
Emily Dimmock	15
Marion Gilchrist	24
"Bible John"	33
Robert Black	38

Britain's Most Depraved Killers

Jon Venables and Robert Thompson   60

Ian Huntley   98

Mick Philpott   154

Dale Cregan   184

Jack Huxley   213

Introduction

A depraved killer who sexually assaulted and murdered his step-grandmother after accessing hardcore pornography was jailed for life in October 2013. Jack Huxley, aged 20, mutilated, stabbed and slashed Janis Dundas 28 times in the bedroom of her Cheshire home. The 62-year-old pensioner was found by police officers face down in a pool of blood with four knives protruding from her back. During sentencing at Liverpool Crown Court, the Recorder of Liverpool, Judge Clement Goldstone, said the killing "plumbed the depths of depravity and brutality". The young killer had spent hours watching porn showing sex between young men and mature women in the hours before and after the murder in Ellesmere Port. As shocking and as vile as the crime was, Huxley is not alone. He is just one of many depraved killers to have committed a heinous murder in Britain.

Throughout history, murderers have made lasting impressions for the crimes they commit. One of Britain's most depraved is Robert Black. In August 1981, nine-year-old Jennifer Cardy pedalled off to see her best friend, riding the red bike her parents had bought her for her birthday two weeks earlier. She never arrived at her destination. Jennifer had ridden straight into the evil clutches of child sex killer Black. Her body was found in a dam almost a week after she vanished. It took 30 years of heartache to bring her killer to justice. In court in 2011, Black was already serving life for three child killings when he was handed another life sentence. Jennifer's family heard sickening details throughout the six-week trial of how Black snatched, abused and killed her. He used his job as a delivery van driver to leave a trail of horror as he criss-crossed Britain. It has always been feared that he killed at least a dozen more children, and police reopened the cold cases of Genette Tate (13), who went missing in Devon in 1978, and April Fabb (13), who disappeared in Norfolk in 1969. It is suspected that both had been riding their bikes along country lanes when they came across Black. He is regarded as one of the most dangerous men in British criminal history, one of 48 UK prisoners who will never be released. In 1990, when Black was caught, a killing spree that had lasted for more than 25 years was brought to an end, but there are many more like Huxley and Black who have darkened Britain's history. James Bulger, who was just short of his third birthday, was murdered in February 1993 by two 10-year-old boys who lured him away from a Liverpool shopping centre while his mother turned her back for a moment.

The boys, Robert Thompson and Jon Venables, led the crying toddler on a two-and-a-half mile walk across the city to Walton. There, on a rarely used piece of railway, they used bricks and sticks to beat and torture him and finally to kill him. CCTV from the shopping centre showed James being led away by the two older boys, who were soon caught. Thompson and Venables were tried and convicted, becoming the youngest murderers ever in British history.

Family doctor Harold Shipman is known to have murdered 218 of his patients, but many believe the total number during his career might have been 355. Shipman, who was 54 when he was caught, worked in Hyde in Cheshire. He dispatched his victims at their own homes with deadly injections of diamorphine. Eighty per cent of his victims were elderly women, but his youngest victim was a man aged only 41. The doctor got away with it for years because he alone signed the death certificates, and because officials were reluctant to believe that a family doctor could be a serial killer. Concerns were first raised about Shipman's activities in 1998 when a local undertaker told police that an unusually large number of his patients were dying; but an initial police investigation cleared him. His undoing came the following year when an elderly patient died: Shipman had altered her will so that he was the beneficiary of her £386,000 estate.

In October 2013, a Gurkha spoke of his grief for his wife who was murdered in a sex attack after her depraved killer was jailed for life.

Thaluman Mabo said that the killing of mother-of-three Krishnamaya Mabo at the hands of Glen Nelson had led to the toughest months of his life.

The proud Gurkha said that dealing with her death had been harder than even the toughest military training he had endured. Nelson, aged 30, was jailed for life and told he would serve a minimum of 25 years after he pleaded guilty to the murder and attempted rape of Krishnamaya as she went for a walk in woodland near her garrison home in Arborfield, Berkshire. The attack, in June that year, was sexually motivated, and prosecutors said that Nelson, who had two previous convictions for attempted rape, was a dangerous offender. In a statement, Mr Mabo, who serves with the Royal Gurkha Rifles, said: "Due to the horrific murder of my wife, life has taken a different path for my family.

"Since the incident, the past few months have been the toughest in my life. The hardest military training seems so much easier compared to what me and my three children have gone through every day. I am proud of my children, the positive way they are coping without the presence of their beloved mother being by their side. I will never know what is going through their thoughts every day. The list could go on and on, but we were determined to get justice because that's what myself, my father, grandfather, forefather, have been fighting for with our British brothers for the last 300 years until now. We are The Gurkhas. In the future I can only hope that in every passing day, we share the memories and live by the morals that were made with my wife, and that her radiating way of life projects through us all in everything my family and I do."

Nelson, who lived in a mobile home in Eversley Road, Arborfield, appeared via videolink at Reading Crown Court to admit his crimes. He had gone out looking for women to attack on the day he murdered Mrs Mabo, 39, but had been scared off by other people or by dogs. The alarm was raised by Mr Mabo when his wife of 20 years did not return home, and she was reported as missing. A volunteer helping with the search found Mrs Mabo's body by a tree in an area known as Long Copse. A post-mortem examination found she died from asphyxiation. Senior Investigating Officer, Detective Chief Inspector Gill Wootton said: "This was a disturbing stranger incident in which a woman walking on her own was attacked and tragically murdered by a man whose actions were clearly sexually motivated." Nelson had already approached a woman earlier the same day and made indecent suggestions and comments towards her.

"Stranger murders like this are an extremely rare occurrence, but when they do happen, they naturally cause a great deal of anxiety and concern," DCI Wootton continued. Following the discovery of Krishnamaya's body, Nelson was swiftly identified as a suspect and was arrested later the same day. When he was interviewed, Nelson initially answered no comment and maintained this position for some time. However, he eventually made a full confession.

"Krishnamaya was a loving wife and mother and her untimely death has had a devastating impact on those close to her, including her family, friends and the wider Nepalese community. I would like to pay tribute to Krishnamaya's family for their wholehearted support of our investigation and I am pleased they have been spared the ordeal of sitting through a trial and can take some comfort in the fact her killer is now behind bars."

Baljit Ubhey, Chief Crown Prosecutor for Thames and Chiltern Crown Prosecution Service (CPS) said: "Mrs Mabo, who had gone out for a walk, had the misfortune to come across Glen Nelson. We may never know for sure what happened, or why Nelson murdered Mrs Mabo, but what we do know is that Nelson is an extremely dangerous man." Nelson received a six-year concurrent sentence for attempted rape.

Despite the fact that many people living in poorer communities at the beginning of the 20th century had little, or no, faith in or respect for the police, the Victorians had a long-held belief that crime could, and would, be beaten. Statistics published throughout the second half of the 19th century alluded to the fact that crime rates were falling. Violent crime was certainly being taken far more seriously than it had been in previous centuries, and perpetrators were severely dealt with by the courts.

By the turn of the 20th century, police forces had been steadily improving for almost 50 years. They were successful in suppressing forms of behaviour that polite society considered offensive and they generally brought about some order and control. However, a number of factors continued to affect crimes throughout the 20th century, including government, war, the economy, beliefs and technology. Britain's industrial supremacy was in decline, with national unemployment reaching 22 per cent by 1933; in parts of Scotland, Wales and northern England, the figures were considerably higher. Statistically, two-thirds of all crimes are committed by males under the age of 25 (females are outnumbered seven to one), while half of all crimes are committed by men under 20 years of age. Young males in the 15–16 age group are most likely to commit a crime. With better health care, increased education and the possibility of greater prosperity throughout the second half of the 20th century and into the 21st century, it is perhaps hard to see why anyone would want to commit a crime – or is it? Lifestyles may have changed and, apart from the fact that Britain has suffered a huge economic downturn since 2008, with crimes involving property and possessions on the increase in a country bound by recession, prosperity is far greater than it was more than 100 years ago. However, in December 2011 unemployment reached a peak, with the highest number of young people out of work for 17 years.

With the suspension and abolition of capital punishment in the second half of the 20th century, deterrents have changed (although serious punishments still exist for the most heinous crimes), but human nature itself is unlikely to change significantly enough to end all crime. Jealousy, greed, obsession, cruelty, fear, state of mind and peer pressure will all still continue to challenge, excite and stimulate those who perpetrate crimes.

Criminals have been perceived by groups in authority and the public in varying different ways throughout history. There were those who would equate a criminal offender as "working class", lazy, prone to drinking and looking for an easy life rather than willing to work for an honest wage. At the turn of the 19th century, others were termed as "dangerous" for taking advantage of disorder within the slums, and up to the early 1900s "criminal classes" was a term all of its own. However, with changes in social understanding and developments in the world of psychiatry, it became increasingly clear that criminals were individuals who were suffering from various forms of behavioural abnormalities brought about by either nature or nurture.

With changing attitudes in almost every aspect of life throughout the 20th century, policing and the public's attitude to the police changed dramatically. At the turn of the century, there were 181 police forces and 60,000 police officers in Britain. Many forces were small, with fewer than 50 policemen, and there was very little collaboration or co-operation between the different forces. There was also no central criminal record base but, slowly, developments began to take place. The use of new technology saw police forces amalgamating, and by the beginning of the new millennium there were 125,000 police officers working in 41 forces across Britain. The job today remains much as it did in 1900, but technology has greatly increased the role of the police, and they now have a far better chance of bringing criminals to justice. New technology, including fingerprinting (developed in 1901) and DNA testing (first reported in 1984 and developed as a process ever since), has created important new ways to identify criminals. Collating information is crucial in identifying perpetrators of crime, and the age of computing opened up huge opportunities for holding and analysing such information. Today, the National Police Computer holds records on more than 25 million people, searchable in a variety of ways. However, despite greater uniformity across police forces (although a Home Office report in December 2011 found that huge improvements could be made in this area), databases, collaboration and technological advances, crimes still blot the landscape of British society. These crimes, especially heinous acts including murder, are particularly upsetting and intolerable, especially, for many, where a killing involves a child.

In May 2013, the *Mirror* said: "Action on internet child pornography [is] long overdue and we have reached the tipping point where something has to be done." The article continued: "If this was a financial problem the best brains around would soon be drafted in to clear things up, so why can't we get the same kind of action to protect children?" Every day police confiscate at least 35,000 images of children suffering horrendous sexual assaults. Some feature babies and toddlers; many involve the young victims in ever more sadistic and perverse sexual acts. Every day someone is charged in court with hoarding thousands, if not millions, of these sordid pictures. The *Mirror* wrote: "As distasteful as this is we should not just see this as a victimless crime being carried out in the privacy of the offender's own home." There is growing evidence that the possession of illegal images and sexual assaults are linked. In the cases of April Jones and Tia Sharp, both their killers, Mark Bridger and Stuart Hazell, had indecent images of children on their computers. A NSPCC study carried out in 2013 found that one in three men found guilty of possessing or downloading these pictures had also committed another sex crime. In 1990, there were an estimated 7,000 hard copies of indecent images in England and Wales. In 2012, five police forces reported they had confiscated 26 million images from offenders. Some progress has been made by industry and government, but efforts "need to be redoubled if we are to make sure the door is slammed shut before there are more tragedies like the murder of April Jones", wrote the newspaper.

The news is constantly full of fatal deaths caused by depraved killers who have little or no thought for their victims. From a murder 900 years ago, unearthed in Scotland in the early part of the 21st century, to the vicious killing of a young beautiful hairdresser in Gloucester in February 2014, murder continues across Britain. In the early part of February 2014 the press announced that archaeologists had discovered a 900-year-old murder victim during a dig at the Scottish Seabird Centre. They found the skeleton of a young man dating from the 12th or 13th century while investigating the historic Kirk Ness, which was the site of a church and cemetery in North Berwick,

East Lothian. Analysis revealed that he was fatally stabbed four times in the back – twice in the left shoulder and twice in the ribs. Archaeologists said he was aged over 20, of slightly better build than average and had wear to his shoulder, suggesting he might have been an archer. The dig, organized by the Scottish Seabird Centre and later supported by Historic Scotland, also revealed structural remains, including stone tools, lead objects, ceramic material and bones of butchered seals, fish and seabirds, which suggested a community lived at the site. The story is fascinating, and thanks to the preservation of the body archaeologists have been able to learn great detail about a bygone way of life, what happened to the victim and the area in which the body was found. Today's murder cases, however, can seem much more disturbing in the quest for the truth.

Hollie Gazzard was named as the young hairdresser who was stabbed to death in Southgate Street, Gloucester on 18th February 2014. The 20-year-old was working at Fringe Benefits & La Bella Beauty salon when she was brutally attacked in front of customers and staff. Neighbours heard shouting and screaming before the suspect fled the scene. Emergency services were called at around 5.50pm and the young woman was rushed to Gloucestershire Royal Hospital, where she later died from her injuries. Detectives launched a manhunt, and a 22-year-old man was arrested on suspicion of murder in the early hours of 19th February. On the local news the night before, a police spokesman called for calm in the Gloucester area, that the man they were looking for was believed to be known to the victim and that her tragic murder was not a random attack. While this news may have eased the shock for those in the local area, it was devastating for those who witnessed the callous stabbing of a young woman in front of staff and customers while she was at work. One woman interviewed by the press said: "It's just awful. To think it can happen in the centre at a busy time makes you feel unsafe." Hollie Gazzard's ex-boyfriend, security guard Asher Maslin, aged 22, was arrested several hours after she was stabbed. He appeared in court not long afterwards. Senior Investigating Officer Detective Chief Inspector Steve Bean said: "I would like to say a personal thank you to everyone who has spoken to us about Hollie's death. We understand this is a case that has affected many people." Hollie's heartbroken parents, Amanda (47) and Nick (49) released a picture of their smiling daughter.

The knife believed to have been used in the attack was found on a building site near the salon where Hollie worked. Her relationship with Maslin ended just four weeks before he killed her. Sadly, this young woman is one of many victims to die at the hands of a depraved killer in Britain.

Murdered Mikaeel Kular's mother was allowed to leave jail to view her son's body in March 2014. Rosdeep Kular, who was accused of murdering the three-year-old, was taken under guard to the funeral home where the little boy's remains were being kept, but she did not attend his funeral.

Guards escorted Kular (33) to an undertaker's in Kirkcaldy. It was understood her mother and stepfather were there. The single mother of five was on remand in Cornton Vale women's prison near Stirling. A source said: "In a situation like that, the governor of the prison would have discretion to agree for an individual to have an escorted release." Police had found Mikaeel's body in woodland in Fife six weeks earlier, after his mother had reported him missing from their home in Edinburgh. She was subsequently charged with his murder and attempting to defeat the ends of justice.

The little boy's funeral took place in Fife on 5th March 2014, led by a female church minister from Edinburgh who had supported the family when Mikaeel disappeared and when his body was discovered.

The *Record* revealed that according to his death certificate Mikaeel died from internal bleeding in his abdomen and from peritonitis. It added that an investigation of the facts of the case was pending. Peritonitis is an inflammation of the peritoneum – the thin lining of the abdomen, or stomach. It is most often caused by an infection from elsewhere but can also develop directly.

Mikaeel's death was registered by his step-grandfather, who signed the document Mr B. Krishnaswamy. The time, date and place of his death were listed as "04.02 on 18 January" in "woodland behind Dunvegan Avenue, Kirkcaldy". The woods were the scene of one of the biggest police forensic operations in Scotland in recent years. Mikaeel's body was found a day after Kular reported him missing from their home in Ferry Gait Crescent, Edinburgh. Hundreds of local people turned out to help police search for the missing toddler. But 36 hours later, the search switched to a home in Kirkcaldy and nearby woodland. Mikaeel's body was found a short time later.

His mother was later charged with his murder and appeared twice in court in Edinburgh, making no plea or declaration. She was remanded in custody after the first appearance.

There are many murderers who have darkened Britain's history. *Britain's Most Depraved Killers* takes a detailed look at some of the most notorious.

Emily Dimmock

Killer unknown (Camden Town Murder, 1907)

The murder of 22-year-old Emily Dimmock became a sensational crime in 1907, in part owing to the theatrical performances that were delivered in the court rooms of the day, and partly because it was a landmark case in legal history. More than 100 years later, the case is still one of the most famous unsolved crimes of the 20th century, following interest from American crime writer Patricia Cornwell and the author's theories concerning Jack the Ripper and artist Walter Sickert.

Emily Dimmock – also known as Mrs Shaw and Phyllis Dimmock – lived at 29 St Paul's Road, near King's Cross, with her partner Bertram "Bert" Shaw, when she was found with her throat cut at her home address on the morning of 12th September. The victim was found in her bedroom lying almost naked across the bed, with a cut to her throat that was so deep it had almost severed her head from her body. In addition, there were odd cuts across both her knees. It was quickly established that owing to a "cast-iron" alibi, Bert Shaw was not a suspect in the case. In fact, Shaw had a job working as a chef for the Midland Railway's night express and was away from home between 4.15pm each afternoon and around 11.30am the following day. He was known to have stayed overnight in Sheffield before travelling back to the capital. Therefore, the police focused their investigation elsewhere.

Dimmock was a young woman who began her working life in service in East Finchley, Hertfordshire. Like many young girls of her generation she found herself in King's Cross, north London, a renowned hotspot for prostitutes and drug dealers alike. Here she lodged with small-time criminal John William Crabtree, who was charged with running a disorderly house just off the Euston Road in Bidborough Street. Dimmock was working as a prostitute when she moved in with Shaw early in 1907. It is known that the young Shaw – he was around 19 years old – was keen for Dimmock to give up her life as a prostitute. By day, Dimmock lived the life that Shaw desired for her, but when he was away at night she returned to her former life of prostitution without his knowledge.

When glass-work designer Robert Wood posted a postcard to "Phyllis" in the early hours of Monday 9th September, signing it "Alice" so as not to arouse Shaw's suspicions, it was to make Wood central to the police case. Dimmock and Wood had met on the previous Friday at the Eagle in Royal College Street. On the postcard he asked Dimmock to meet him at 8.15pm at the Rising Sun (he actually drew a rising sun). Meanwhile, Dimmock spent three nights in a row with ship's cook Robert Percival Roberts. When she turned up at the Eagle on the evening of Wednesday 11th September, not far away in the Rising Sun Roberts was drinking with his friend Frank Clarke; the two men were expecting Dimmock to meet them. Dimmock was seen by several witnesses while she was drinking with Wood. Roberts would later testify that it was on the morning of the day before she died that the victim showed him a letter folded in four. It was reportedly from Bert Shaw, asking her to meet him that evening in the Eagle in Camden Town at 8.30pm, but the writing proved similar to that of Wood's postcard and the charred remains ultimately proved indecipherable to the police. The drinking session with Wood was to be the last time Emily Dimmock was seen alive.

The following morning, Bert Shaw's mother travelled from Northampton to her son's rooms to meet Emily. Mrs Shaw was less than pleased with her son's involvement with the young prostitute and the visit was not a social one. Mrs Shaw arrived at the house well before her son's shift on the night express had ended and knocked on the door. There was no answer. A neighbour, Mrs Stocks, allowed Shaw's mother to sit in the passage to wait for her son, who then borrowed a key to enter the rooms. It was then that the three of them discovered Emily's bloodstained body.

It was clear to the two shocked women and Bert Shaw that the rooms had been ransacked – Dimmock's postcard collection had been wrecked (Wood's postcard was not found at the scene), and whoever had murdered the victim had clearly washed their hands in the washbasin in the bedroom. When the police arrived they quickly began to piece together Dimmock's life while Shaw was away. Bert eventually found the postcard which Emily Dimmock had carefully hidden when he moved rooms and was clearing out her belongings. Wood was soon identified as the author. At best, the evidence against the designer was circumstantial, and many men – particularly soldiers and sailors known to the victim – were questioned about the crime.

Two days after the murder, newspaper reports confirmed that a man's bloodstained handkerchief (showing a laundry mark) was retrieved by police from the crime scene, along with a crumpled letter found under the bed and the charred remains of other correspondence in the fireplace. Reports also stated that many bloodstained fingerprints in the bedroom were found on the bedclothes, the bedposts and the washbasin. The technique of fingerprinting was in early development and it was far too soon to use the process. "The room was in disorder, as if there had been a struggle" was the official description of the scene, and it was this along with the fact that jewellery belonging to the victim worth up to £10 had been stolen that led police to believe initially that the motive had been robbery. However, the evidence possibly suggested something more sinister. Dimmock was found on the bed in a sleeping position; there were no defensive wounds to her arms and her hair had been pulled to one side. It has been medically proven that it is difficult to cut a throat when the victim is struggling, so it seemed likely that Dimmock was totally unaware she was about to be attacked, suggesting that she was asleep between 3.00am and 6.00am when, following examination of her stomach contents, the murder was deduced to have taken place.

Four days after the murder, newspaper reports talked about "important developments in connection with the grim mystery" and stated that police, led by Assistant Commissioner Macnaghten and Superintendent Vedy, "are confident that they will be able to make an arrest before many hours have passed". Despite the victim's postcard collection being wrecked on the night of the tragedy, the postcards that remained were proving helpful to police in their quest for the murderer. By this time, they no longer suspected that robbery was the motive, and jealousy or revenge were cited in the daily newspapers as new possible motives. The inquest was opened at noon on 16th September at St Pancras Coroner's Court. Despite reports that the authorities were close to an arrest, by 23rd September no arrest had yet been made, although detectives were convinced they knew the identity of the killer. However, on 7th October 1907, the police made an arrest. It was reported in the *Daily Mirror* that "they have taken into custody Robert Thomas William George Cavers Wood, aged about 29". Wood was brought before Clerkenwell Police Court that same day.

Wood's arrest took place after the *Daily Mirror* suggested to Scotland Yard that the postcards written to the victim should be reproduced in the daily newspapers. The handwriting on one of the postcards was recognized by Ruby Young, a former girlfriend of Wood's, who mentioned it to a friend. Young and Wood met following the reproduction of the postcards in the news and he admitted that he knew Dimmock, although he was adamant that he was not with her on the night she was murdered. Young's friend had a journalist friend, who arranged for Ruby to speak to Detective Inspector Neill, who was in overall charge of the case.

When arrested, Wood, from King's Cross, admitted that he had written the postcard making an appointment with Emily Dimmock at the Rising Sun on the night before she was murdered. He denied that a further three cards sent to Dimmock were anything to do with him. He gave a full account of his movements the night Emily was murdered, and claimed to have first heard of the murder two days after it was committed. Wood also stated that he had only ever met the victim twice, and that he didn't even know her name. He said that he had written the postcard to Phyllis at her request, after offering it to her instead of the postcards that were being sold by a young boy in the pub, and that also at her request he signed it "Alice", "in case my old man should see it". The appointment, Wood claimed, was bogus. He stated that he saw Dimmock again a few days later on Monday 9th September, both in the Rising Sun and later the same evening when she was stopped by a group of men.

Wood's younger brother backed up his account of what happened on the Wednesday night. "He was a methodical man" who always "returned home between 10.30pm and midnight." He claimed that Wood never changed this routine, so it would have been impossible for him to be out when the victim was attacked. Despite having an alibi, though, Wood was charged on 7th October 1907 with murder, and remanded for eight days when bail was refused by the magistrate.

The inquest resumed on 14th October 1907. Bert Shaw was the first to give evidence. He confirmed that various pieces of jewellery had gone missing from the property on the night of the murder, along with three keys. Shaw also stated the times of the trains he took to and from Sheffield on the days in question and was able to prove his alibi. Detective Inspector Neill was the next witness. It was stated that Wood alleged that the first time he met Dimmock was on Friday 6th September, just six days before the murder. The inquest was adjourned for a week and Wood was once again remanded in custody.

The New Bailey's public gallery was filled with many actors, writers and artists of the day, as keen to see the renowned and high-profile Edward Marshall Hall QC in action defending Wood as they were to see the accused himself. Marshall Hall was loved by the crowd, who hung onto his every word, despite the fact that the case for Wood's defence was somewhat bizarre and varied. Wood had gone to extraordinary lengths to ensure his alibi for the evening of 11th September, and Robert McCowan – a witness for the prosecution – was asked to recount the events surrounding the man he had seen leaving 29 St Paul's Road at around 4.55am on the fateful morning of 12th September. McCowan believed he saw the accused leaving the premises with his collar upturned, wearing a hard bowler hat, with a slightly jerky walk and his left hand in his pocket. (Following a childhood accident resulting in a damaged finger, Wood was known for keeping his hand out of sight.) However, despite the fact that witnesses swore that the man they saw was Wood because of the manner of his walk, and the fact that John Crabtree also swore under oath that Wood had previously visited his premises several times in Bidborough Street, the case rested on visibility. As much as the prosecution said they could bring in witnesses to say Wood had a distinctive walk, Marshall Hall claimed he could bring in just as many to say he didn't.

Marshall Hall defended that when McCowan walked down St Paul's Road it would have been impossible to tell without close inspection that the man he saw was in fact not Wood at all. William Westcott, a keen boxer with a swing to his walk, and also a resident of St Paul's Road, was on an early shift at St Pancras that morning, and was in the road at the same time as McCowan. Marshall Hall argued that it was Westcott that McCowan had seen and not the accused. The point about the distinctive walk was conceded. Even though Marshall Hall's summing up was excellent, he still felt that Wood could be convicted of the crime. However, the judge instructed the jury that the prosecution had an unproven case, and after deliberating for 15 minutes a "not guilty" verdict was returned.

Wood was the first accused man in a murder trial to give evidence on his own behalf following the Criminal Justice Bill of 1905. It was a landmark case in English legal history, even though it seems likely that Wood lied under oath – if Crabtree and other prostitutes were telling the truth about his association with Dimmock – and he was an unreliable witness.

Marion Gilchrist

Killer unknown (1908)

Aged 82, Marion Gilchrist was fully in charge of her faculties. Given her age, the spinster, who shared her home with her live-in maid Helen Lambie, was somewhat absent-minded at times and frail but nevertheless relatively healthy. She was known to have worried about the possibility of burglars and kept the outer door to her flat in the residential quarter of Queen's Terrace, Glasgow locked at all times. The year was 1908 and Glasgow's reputation for gang crime and frequent murders was notorious. Most of the city's underbelly of crime was a world away from the life that Gilchrist lived, but her nervousness about the possibility of being robbed led her to joke to her neighbour in the flat below that should she ever need help she would knock three times on the floor. In fact, she had done this on previous occasions when she felt something was wrong, and her good friend and neighbour Arthur Adams had looked in on the fastidious and cultured Gilchrist to check up. But, apart from the fact that the elderly lady's dog had been mysteriously poisoned some months before, nothing had ever been amiss.

On the evening of 21st December 1908, Helen Lambie left her employer reading at the dining table as she headed out of No. 15 just before 7.00pm to buy the evening papers. In the 10 minutes it would take before the young woman returned,

Gilchrist was to suffer a savage and shocking attack which left her dead in a pool of blood, sparking events that led to a notorious miscarriage of justice and a cover-up by the authorities.

It was assumed that the motive for the attack was robbery. Gilchrist was a wealthy woman who, it was established, had a number of pieces of jewellery hidden in her wardrobe. At around 7.00pm on the night of the attack, Adams was relaxing at home with his sister when he heard knocking on the ceiling of his apartment. As there were more than three he wasn't unduly concerned, but decided in any case to check on the elderly lady. Hovering outside her door, Adams heard a noise which sounded like the maid breaking sticks. As he was unaware that Lambie wasn't at home, he went back down to his own apartment, before being persuaded by his sister to go back upstairs and check once more on Gilchrist. Adams arrived back at the flat's door at about the same time as Lambie, and as the maid unlocked the door, a stranger calmly walked past them both. It only took a few seconds for Lambie to find her employer lying in the dining room, battered about the head and upper body. The victim was barely alive, and died within seconds of being found, at which point Lambie cried out : "My mistress is murdered ... catch that man!"

According to newspaper reports at the time, the man did not arouse any suspicion as he calmly walked by but, on hearing Lambie's cries from the dining room, Adams flew after him and "ran down the stairs almost at the heels of the man, but the stranger fled and was soon out of reach". The street outside was ill-lit, with many opportunities to fade away into the darkness. Adams was very unlikely to see or to be able to catch the elderly spinster's attacker. However, 15-year-old Mary Barrowman had also seen a man in the vicinity of Queen's Terrace on the night of the murder and she was questioned by police about the suspect as well.

Back at the flat, even though a large quantity of Gilchrist's valuable diamonds were lodged with her jewellers in Glasgow, there were still many thousands of pounds worth of jewellery on the premises. Although the police were convinced the motive was robbery, only an expensive diamond brooch was missing. However, the intruder had managed to force open a box in the victim's bedroom and a number of papers, rings and gold watches were found on the floor. It appeared that the murderer was more interested in the victim's private papers, which had been locked away.

Gilchrist was popular and had a wide circle of friends, and the police, fearing a public outcry, were keen to act quickly. The fact that her dog had been poisoned before the fateful night led the authorities to believe that the attack was premeditated.

Both Adams and Lambie gave a description of the suspect to police, and when five days later the police were tipped off about a diamond brooch being pawned by a man living nearby, they were confident that they had their man. Oscar Slater – originally Oscar Leschnizer – was a German Jew who had fled to

Glasgow in order to avoid military conscription. The fact that his life was particularly sordid (he was a pimp, trafficker of stolen jewellery and gambler) did little to help his cause with the police. Armed with their tip-off about the brooch, when police arrived at Slater's home they discovered that he had recently left Scotland, bound for New York on the *Lusitania*, using a false name – Otto Sando – and with his mistress Andree Antoine. With these new revelations, the police were more convinced than ever that Slater was the man for whom they were looking.

When the vessel docked in New York, Slater was arrested for murder by local detectives, who found a diamond brooch in the suspect's pocket. Adams, Lambie and Barrowman then crossed the Atlantic in order to identify Slater. Both Lambie and Barrowman claimed that Slater could have been the man they had seen on the night of the murder, although Adams was less sure. Despite the fact that extradition proceedings were started, Oscar Slater was so convinced that he wouldn't be convicted of a crime of which he steadfastly maintained he was innocent that he returned to Scotland of his own free will. It was to prove a huge mistake for the 37-year-old, who found that anti-Jewish sentiment and his lifestyle would go against him. There were 98 witnesses for the prosecution when Slater came to trial in Edinburgh in early May 1909. Although Helen Lambie had not been totally convinced in New York that Slater was the man she had seen, by the time the case came to trial the maidservant was adamant that the man she had seen on the night in question was the German. The case was further strengthened by evidence from a Constable Buen, who claimed to have seen Slater "in the street near Miss Gilchrist's house at about 9.00pm about a week before the murder". This was perhaps unsurprising as Slater lived about four roads away from Gilchrist, but that was never mentioned at the time.

The Lord Advocate, Alexander Ure, was convinced that Slater should hang, and the jury were under no illusion that they should find the man before them, "with a twisted nose" as he was described at the time by Detective Trench, guilty. Slater was indeed found guilty by the 15-strong jury and sentenced to death by hanging on 27th May 1909. The fact that the brooch in Slater's pocket was his own and not that of the dead woman, the fact that he had been invited to America by a friend and the fact that he had changed his name in order to avoid his estranged wife had little or no sway in his case. A further point that indicated the trial had been a travesty was that it was quite obvious that Gilchrist was so nervous that she would never have opened her door to a stranger. The attacker must have been someone the victim knew, as there was no sign of forced entry, yet Slater and the murdered lady were unknown to each other. Marion Gilchrist had been battered to death in her own home, her head bashed in "with lightning-like rapidity" between 20 and 40 times, and someone would pay. That someone was Slater.

The death of Marion Gilchrist and the subsequent arrest and conviction of Slater caused a sensation throughout Scotland

and beyond. Rumours were rife, including that Slater was actually Gilchrist's long-lost son or that the victim had been a resetter (a receiver of stolen uncut diamonds). All these rumours were identified as false and unfounded, but the case was mysterious and causing unrest and speculation, which the police were eager to quash.

Almost as soon as Slater was sentenced to death, a petition for clemency was started on his behalf and more than 20,000 signatures were collated. Just one day before the death penalty was to be carried out, Slater's sentence was reduced to life imprisonment and he was transferred to Peterhead jail. Slater maintained his innocence, and some of his friends approached the author Sir Arthur Conan Doyle to see if his influence might help achieve justice for the convicted man. Conan Doyle had read about the case in *Notable Scottish Trials* and was appalled that Slater had been convicted on such flimsy circumstantial evidence and suspicion, but getting the case back into public interest turned out to be a slow and lengthy process. Conan Doyle's book *The Case of Oscar Slater*, published three years after Slater's conviction, brought about numerous demands for a pardon or retrial, but authorities refused to change the status quo. It seemed that Slater had very little choice but to wait out his days in prison. However, he was not forgotten by those convinced of his innocence and, over the next 15 years, various facts were uncovered which would lead to his eventual release and pardon.

When Conan Doyle re-examined all the evidence presented at the trial, he found it surprising that Lambie did not react at all when she was passed in the corridor of the flat by the attacker. It seemed clear that she had known the assailant, and had possibly been surprised to see him in her mistress' home; however, she was not panicked by the presence of the man, which led Conan Doyle to suspect that she knew all too well that it was not Slater. He found other witnesses, including Duncan McBrain, who saw Slater outside his own flat at the time of the murder, and 30-year-old Agnes Brown, who actually saw the murderer leaving Miss Gilchrist's building. It was not Oscar Slater. However, neither of these witnesses was called to testify at Slater's trial. Conan Doyle wanted to know why.

Central to the police's case was that it was Slater's name and description in the paper that prompted the convicted man to flee Glasgow under a false name. However, Conan Doyle discovered that not only had Slater booked passage for himself and his mistress some six weeks before the murder, but that he was already on his way to New York when the paper was published. At the trial, a jewel hammer was presented as evidence of the murder weapon, but Conan Doyle was unconvinced that such a weapon could have caused such devastating injuries. Furthermore, Dr Adams, who was called to the scene on the night of 21st December 1908 – and was also never called to give evidence – found that the weapon most likely to have been used was one of the victim's dining room chairs. The left back leg and front right leg of the chair were found at the scene to have brain, hairs and blood stuck to them, a fact that was never introduced at court. Dr Adams quickly deduced that the murderer knocked Miss Gilchrist to the ground, picked up the chair in which she had been sitting and hit her with it five or six times. Considering the injuries suffered by the victim, the doctor was also fairly confident that the murderer had jumped up and down on the body, such was the frenzied nature of the attack. What Conan Doyle also discovered was that when the forensic scientists arrived the following morning to work the crime scene, the dining chair had been cleaned; it had also been moved back to its original position, where the victim had been sitting. It was police procedure at the time to preserve all evidence at the crime scene so, while it was possible to concede that the chair had been moved accidentally, it looked as if the chair had been cleaned.

Conan Doyle was also keen to re-examine the testimony of Helen Lambie, because it was clear that between seeing Slater in New York and seeing him again at the trial she had changed her witness statement. Conan Doyle also questioned the prosecution's attempts to link Slater with the man, described as a "watcher", who had been spotted outside the flat on several occasions leading up to the murder. Around 20 people identified Slater with varying degrees of certainty as the man who had been seen outside before the attack, but many of these so-called witnesses contradicted each other and Conan

Doyle concluded that this evidence was a farce. Detective Trench eventually admitted that he had never believed Miss Lambie's identification of Slater, and was sacked without pension for leaking documents to the press which hinted at a conspiracy.

Finally, after serving 18 years in prison for a murder he did not commit, Oscar Slater was pardoned by the Scottish Court of Criminal Appeal when all the new evidence was presented to the authorities.

For some time after the events, it was thought that Miss Gilchrist's nephew Dr Francis Charteris had killed her, but another candidate might be Wingate Birrell, fiancé of Helen Lambie. However, it was also known that Helen Lambie was expected to "make herself scarce" when Miss Gilchrist had business visitors, who were fairly "shady" acquaintances who called to do business with her regarding valuable jewellery of not altogether legitimate provenance.

"Bible John"

(1968–69)

Convicted of double rape in 1993, violent and sadistic Peter Tobin spent 10 years in prison for sexual attacks on two young girls whom he had held at knifepoint, forcing them to drink strong alcohol before he turned on the gas taps and left them for dead. The victims survived and Tobin, who then went on the run, was caught hiding out with a religious sect in the West Midlands. His life up to this point had been littered with crime and violence against women. The youngest of seven children, Tobin had been sent to an approved school at the tender age of seven because he was an extremely difficult child, who obviously had major problems that his family was unable to cope with.

Tobin was released from jail in 2004 after serving his time for the double rape but, just three years later, was sentenced to life – with the recommendation to serve a minimum of 21 years – for the rape and murder of Angelika Kluk, which he committed in 2006 in Glasgow. He was subsequently found guilty of the murders of two other women, who had gone missing in 1991, when their remains were found at his former home in Margate, Kent. His minimum sentence was extended to 30 years. There has been much speculation that Tobin is the serial killer "Bible John" who killed three women in the Glasgow area in the late 1960s. But is he?

Patricia Docker's body was found on 23rd February 1968. The 25-year-old had been strangled, but the police investigation was hampered when two months after Patricia's death it was discovered that she had been at the Barrowland Ballroom and not the Majestic Ballroom, as she had told her parents the night before she died. In August 1969, there were rumours that children playing in an old building in MacKeith Street had seen the body of a woman. These were dismissed as a wild fantasy on the part of the children, but 32-year-old Jemima McDonald was missing after a night out at Barrowland Ballroom and her sister was concerned enough to go and see for herself. What she found was the battered body of the mother of three, who had been raped, strangled and beaten to death. When the police began their investigation, it was discovered that Jemima had been seen leaving the dance hall at about midnight with a tall, slim man with reddish hair. A third victim also visited the Barrowland Ballroom that year.

On 30th October, 29-year-old Helen Puttock went to the club with her sister Jean. The two women met a couple of men at the club, both called John. After spending more than an hour together, the foursome left the club and one of the men headed for a bus in George Square. Helen, Jean and the second man got in a taxi together. In the Scotstoun area, Jean got out of the taxi believing that it was bound for Helen's home in Earl Street and that her sister was safe. The following morning, Helen's battered body was found in the back garden of her flat. Like

Patricia, Helen had been raped and strangled. Her handbag had been rifled and the contents strewn nearby but the actual bag was missing. Helen had a deep bitemark on her leg.

By this time, although there was no concrete evidence that the killer was the same man who had murdered Patricia and Jemima, the police thought it highly likely. The man that Jean met said his name was John "Templeton" or "Sempleson" and repeatedly quoted from the Bible. She described him as tall and slim with reddish to fair hair. Jean stated to police that the man was well dressed, young, extremely polite and well spoken. He had told Jean the night before that he believed dance halls were dens of iniquity. However, other witnesses – including the bouncers at the club – described the man as short with black hair, and a further witness had also heard him describe Barrowland as a "den of iniquity". Jean was incredibly drunk the night she left the club with Helen and the man calling himself John, so it is possible that her description was inaccurate. At around 1.30am on the night Helen was killed, a young smartly dressed man fitting the description of "Bible John" was seen heading towards the north side of the River Clyde ferry.

Police were determined to catch "Bible John", but they had very little to go on. The first victim, Patricia, hadn't been where they thought she was, so witnesses were unable to give much information by the time the police tracked them down. Jemima's night out at Barrowland Ballroom didn't throw up any significant clues, and Jean's description of the killer was possibly unreliable. Despite this, a number of suspects were questioned, but no arrests were made. Interestingly, all three victims had been menstruating at the time they were murdered, and tampons and other sanitary products were placed on or near the three women. Each woman's handbag was also missing, which led the police to believe that the killer had taken them as a trophy, and all three had been strangled with their own stockings.

Years after the murders, police exhumed the body of former Scots Guard John Irvine McInnes from his grave in Lanarkshire in order to test for DNA matches on Helen's tights on which semen had been found. The tests, carried out in 1996, proved inconclusive. However, there were striking similarities between the murders in Glasgow in 1968 and 1969 and that of Angelika Kluk, a Polish student who was on a working holiday in Glasgow at the time of her death. She was last seen in the company of Tobin who, calling himself Pat McLaughlin, was working at St Patrick's Roman Catholic Church as a handyman. He was using a different name to avoid detection by police and the probation service, given that he was a registered sex offender following his conviction for the double rape. Police knew that Tobin's three former wives had been subjected to violent treatment at his hands: all three had been raped by him and severely beaten as well as being imprisoned; Tobin had also throttled all three on more than one occasion. In addition, there are striking similarities between Tobin's appearance and that of an artist's impression of "Bible John" drawn in the 1960s.

Tobin had been living in Glasgow at the end of the 1960s and had moved from the city in 1969 following his first marriage. He met his first wife at Barrowland Ballroom in 1969, and it is known that he was driven to violence by a woman's menstrual cycle. This had long been suspected by police as being the motive behind the "Bible John" killings.

Helen's sister, Jean McLachlan, died in 2010 at the age of 74; she was the only known woman to have seen "Bible John" close up, and although DNA might prove Tobin's guilt for the three murders, police believe that poor storage of any samples make this virtually impossible. There are those who don't believe all three women were murdered by "Bible John"; some believe that the first murder of Patricia Docker could have been carried out by a different man. But the evidence suggests that in all likelihood these three cruel murders were perpetrated by one killer, and many believe that the man responsible is Peter Tobin.

Robert Black

(1969 and beyond)

A massive police hunt got underway on Saturday 19th August 1978 when 13-year-old Genette Tate simply cycled into thin air. The newspaper girl was last seen by two schoolfriends, who confirmed that she stopped to chat for a moment before pedalling around the corner of a country lane in Aylesbeare, near Exeter, Devon on her afternoon round. Just minutes later, Genette's friends found her bike abandoned in the middle of the road surrounded by newspapers. More than 100 police officers and 50 villagers took part in the search as fears grew for the young girl's safety. To start with, Detective Chief Superintendent Sharpe, head of Devon and Cornwall CID, kept an open mind, although he admitted that the search was on the same scale as a murder hunt. But the case was a complete mystery: there was no sign of an accident or a struggle at the spot where the bike was found.

John Tate, Genette's 36-year-old father, was anguished when the press spoke to him at the family cottage. He was sure that his daughter would not have run away, and said that it just wasn't the sort of thing Genette would do. He appealed to anyone who might have abducted his daughter to return her safely to her family. Friends Tracey Pratt (14) and Margaret Heavy (12) told how they had last seen the missing girl moments before they found her blue and white bike. Although the newspapers Genette had been carrying were scattered everywhere, the two girls were confident that if their missing friend had been attacked and had screamed they would have heard her.

The mystery was heightened by Chief Superintendent Reginald Lester, head of Norfolk CID, who linked the case with that of another missing girl, April Fabb, who vanished in April 1969. April, also 13, went missing on a country lane while riding her blue and white bike in a case that continued to baffle police. As in Genette's case, there were only a few minutes between when the girl was last seen and when her abandoned bike was found. Lester said at the time that the situation defied belief: "I have never known anything like it. A child has quite literally disappeared – in broad daylight, only yards from her home." April went missing in the tiny hamlet of Metton, Norfolk. Known to be shy and timid, she was on holiday from Cromer Secondary School, and was looking forward to going to Norwich to buy some material for her sewing class. By 10.00am on the day she disappeared, April was dressed in brown trousers and a green jumper. At 12.20pm, she returned from walking the family's Cairn terrier, Trudy. Twenty minutes later, she was given a note from a friend, Susan Dixon, who was unable to make the shopping trip the following day. April was upset and, at her mother's suggestion, headed for the nearby telephone box to phone her friend Gillian Smith to see if she could go instead. At

1.30pm she was back from the telephone box, with the answer that Gillian would be able to go into Norwich with her. As April was much happier, her mother suggested she should take the cigarettes she was giving her brother-in-law, Bernard, for his birthday to his home in a neighbouring village. Her mother gave her a blue handkerchief to go with the cigarettes. April went upstairs to change into a red divided skirt; her hair was up in a brown bow and she was wearing slip-on Scholl sandals. At around 1.40pm, April got on her bike and cycled 200 yards down the road in the direction of her sister Pam's house in Roughton, two and a half miles away. Before she had travelled far, the shy girl stopped and spoke to two friends, Christine Dixon and Maureen Hueck, both aged 12. The girls were playing in a field when April stopped to talk, but she was soon on her way to her sister's. At around six minutes past two, she was spotted by tractor driver Joseph Livingston-Brown and other witnesses just by Pill Box crossroads. By 2.15pm, the blue and white bike was seen about 150 yards past the crossroads by three men working for the Ordnance Survey, but they thought nothing of it and drove on. The bike had been thrown into a field, and April had by then been missing for nine minutes. In due course the bike was spotted by a local man, David Empson, and taken to Roughton Police Station. The cigarettes and handkerchief along with some small change were found in the saddlebag. Meanwhile, April's parents had their evening meal, a little put out that their daughter had stayed at her sister's for tea without letting them know. By 7.00pm, however, her mother was beginning to worry. April's father thought that his son-in-law would bring his daughter home at any minute, but at 8.30pm his wife set off on her own bicycle for Pam's house. Fifteen minutes later, Mrs Fabb learned that her youngest daughter had never arrived, and police were involved in an investigation by 10 o'clock that evening. The question was asked, where is April Fabb? It's a question that is still being asked today. There is every possibility that she rode into the clutches of child-killer Robert Black.

On the day she went missing, Genette Tate was doing a favour for a friend by delivering the evening newspapers. In an emotional appeal, her mother Sheila and stepmother Violet buried their differences and begged whomever was holding Genette to let her go. Four days after the girl went missing, three of her friends joined in the hunt and made a dramatic reconstruction of the girl's last known movements. Both Tracey and Margaret retraced their steps of Saturday 19th August, while another friend, known only as Amanda, rode Genette's bike. She admitted to being very nervous, but said she desperately wanted to help find her best friend. Ten days after the incident, police issued a photofit of a man they wanted to interview. He had been seen driving a maroon car close to the spot where the missing girl vanished and the police, led by Detective Chief Superintendent Eric Rundle, were convinced he had vital information. The car had passed Genette and her friends –

travelling in the same direction as the schoolgirl – before she cycled around the bend in the lane. The driver was described as between 18 and 25 years old with thick blackish eyebrows and a pale complexion; he was wearing a light coloured suit with rolled up sleeves. But, despite appeals combined with a search by more than 7,000 volunteers, Genette's disappearance remained a mystery.

Almost two years after Genette's disappearance her family was still in turmoil. By February 1980, her father and stepmother had separated as the pain of their loss continued to be too much to bear. The pressures had been building up for the Tate family, and there was still no news about what had happened to Genette. John Tate and his second wife, Violet, had already founded the International Find A Child organization to help families of missing children, and it was hoped that the charity wouldn't fold owing to the couple's separation. But the family's anguish didn't end with the Tates' divorce. In May the same year, it was revealed that Genette had been a desperately unhappy child, and police began to wonder whether she had simply just run away from home. She had shown her distress by slashing furniture and starting a fire, and a senior police officer gave an interview to the press in which he stated that it was possible she had run away, although the official police line was that she was most likely to have been abducted.

In 1986, it was suggested at a unique crisis summit of police chiefs in London, following the horrific murder of 10-year-old schoolgirl Sarah Harper, that one man or a group of men was responsible for abducting, abusing, killing and disposing of a number of children. Genette was one of the victims on the list, along with Susan Lawrence (14), who went missing from her London home in July 1979, and Martin Allen (15), who disappeared on 5th November that same year. There were 14 other cases listed, including Susan Maxwell (11), murdered in July 1982, and five-year-old Caroline Hogg, found murdered in July 1983. Several factors linked many of the cases together, including the following: a car was used, there was powerful sexual assault, the body was dumped some miles from the victim's home and the perpetrator was quick, clever, ruthless and cool.

There had been several suspects in the frame for the abduction – and by now the murder – of Genette, but none had been convicted. By the mid-1990s, a new man was under suspicion. Robert Black became notorious as Britain's worst serial child-killer, who boasted about the 40 young girls he had cruelly abused in the years before he turned to murder. He was questioned by police about Genette and gave details to Channel 4's *Dispatches* programme about how the 13-year-old was grabbed from her bike and bundled into a vehicle. The former van driver gave chilling accounts of the young girls he had killed, and said: "Somebody once said to me that their motto was 'When they're big enough, they are old enough.' I tended to agree with that. I love children but I don't want to hurt them. Therefore, if I don't want to hurt them they'd have to be dead." Black turned out to be the killer of Susan Maxwell, Caroline Hogg and Sarah Harper. Having been convicted, he was sentenced to 10 life sentences and directed to serve a minimum of 35 years, while the mothers of all three girls sobbed in the public gallery. The 47-year-old Black showed no emotion in court and only spoke when he sneered "Well done, boys" to police officers as he was led away. Although Black's conviction brought a little comfort to the grieving families of Susan, Caroline and Sarah, he refused to see John Tate who desperately wanted to know if Genette had also been a victim. It was 18 years since the abduction and Tate could find no rest, even though Black was suspected of other unsolved crimes. Black sent a terse note to Tate: "I have nothing to say." He later denied any involvement in Genette's disappearance. However, years later Black was again quizzed by police, who had long suspected that he was involved.

In 2003, 25 years after Genette disappeared, her family and the police were convinced that she was dead, yet the case remained open and hope was still held out that her killer would be found. In April 2005, Black was arrested while in prison on suspicion of murdering Genette, and was taken for questioning at a top-security police station in Leeds. He had twice before been interviewed in prison and refused to answer questions, so Home Office permission was granted for him to be removed from jail for questioning. But there was insufficient evidence linking Black to the murder, and in 2008 the collapse of the case against the Scottish van driver dealt a devastating blow to the Tate family and the police. In 2011, Black was still the prime suspect for the killing of Genette and April Fabb, and was suspected of killing at least 12 more children in the UK and France before his capture in 1990.

The biggest ever missing persons inquiry that Britain had ever seen, a £1,000 reward offered in 1978 for information and 7,000 members of the public desperately trying to help trace the missing schoolgirl all failed to turn up any clues that would lead to what had happened to the elfin-faced teenager. The case remains open, and while it has long been suspected that Genette Tate is sadly no longer alive, the hope that her killer will one day be identified lives on. Black was at least convicted for other murders.

In March 1992, Black was charged with the murder of the three schoolgirls, Susan Maxwell, Caroline Hogg and Sarah Harper, during the previous 10 years. Their bodies were found near the M1 motorway. Summonses were issued against the man from Stamford Hill, North London at Newcastle-upon-Tyne Magistrates' Court. He was also charged with the kidnap of Teresa Thornhill (15). A nine-year hunt was launched after the body of Susan Maxwell was found in a layby at Uttoxeter, Staffordshire in 1982. She had vanished as she returned home at Cornhill-on-Tweed in Scotland after a tennis game. The body of the dark-haired Girl Guide was discovered 240 miles away.

Next to vanish was Caroline Hogg, from the Edinburgh suburb of Portobello. The fair-haired little girl was last seen at a seaside funfair in July 1983. Her naked body was found 10 days later in a layby ditch near Twycross in Leicestershire. Three years later, in March 1986, Sarah Harper disappeared as she ran to buy a loaf of bread in Morley, Leeds. Her body was found 23 days later in the River Trent, near Nottingham. Teenager Teresa Thornhill was allegedly bundled into a car at Radford, Nottingham, but escaped. Between February and March 1992, Black was questioned by police in Alnwick, Northumberland.

He was described as Britain's most depraved child-killer, an evil pervert, who gave his chilling account in tape-recorded interviews broadcast on TV 13 hours after he was finally caged for murdering the three children he snatched from the streets. At the time, it was thought he might have murdered 12 more young girls. Detectives were literally queuing to interview him. What was clear was that his assaults spanned more than 30 years. The driver said: "If there was a girl on her own when I was delivering I'd like to sit down and talk to her for a few minutes and try to touch her. Sometimes I succeeded, sometimes not." He described his twisted logic: "In my mind the ideal situation would be a child that was completely willing and eager." Black's job delivering advertising posters took him on frequent long-distance trips, giving him ample opportunity to roam the country looking for young girls. He targeted those with bare legs and wearing white ankle socks. He was able to target areas where he was a complete stranger, bundling his victims into his grubby van before racing to the "Midlands triangle", where the three bodies were dumped within 24 miles of each other. Right to the end, Black continued to deny the murders. But TV interviews with him gave an insight into his depraved mind. These were conducted by psychologist Ray Wyre while Black was in prison in Scotland for the 1990 abduction of a six-year-old girl. He was asked when he first got the idea of snatching a child and the convicted killer started to talk about a newspaper girl. When asked if he meant Genette, Black said: "Yes." He gave permission for the interviews to be used, but talked about Genette's kidnapper in the third person. "He's obviously persuaded her to get off her bike or grabbed her off her bike – one of the two. Then he got her into a vehicle and took her away." He added: "If I seen a paper girl, like I'd maybe park and watch for a while to see what sort of route … getting myself into a position where it would be possible to take somebody." He went on to say that his criminal activities had begun with an assault on a seven-year-old girl in Scotland in 1963, when he was 16. He lured her into an old air raid shelter by promising to show her a kitten. "She started to cry. I think I clapped my hands over her mouth. I took her inside and I held her down on the ground with my hand round her throat and I was holding her down and she must have gone unconscious." Black told Wyre that he sometimes thought of his victims being "unconscious, or drunk, or drugged or something like that". Wyre deduced that the murderer's reasoning seemed crazy, adding: "But in his rationale and his thinking it appeared to become an essential part of allowing him to carry out this re-offending."

Black was convicted of nine charges related to the three murders and for kidnapping Teresa. The child porn addict was described by judge Mr Justice Macpherson of Cluny as a "very dangerous man" and was locked up in isolation at Durham jail – segregated for his own safety after receiving death threats from other prisoners. The judge told him: "I expect you will be detained for the whole of your life."

Susan Maxwell was the first of his victims to die, snatched near her farmhouse home on 30th July 1982. She was walking alone for the first time after playing tennis in Coldstream. In the summer heat, Black's fantasies become a brutal reality. Following the murders of Caroline and Sarah, police from six forces took more than 175,000 statements and checked tens of thousands of car registrations during the eight-year probe, which cost £12 million. Black told police nothing about the killings, but at one point he asked to be allowed to send letters to the grieving parents, saying: "Don't blame yourselves – there is nothing you could have done." Prison officers were so stunned by his callousness that they tore up the letters. Before his trial he was switched from Peterhead on Scotland's bleak north-east coast to Durham. He wanted to get back to Peterhead, though, where he joined the five-a-side football team, the weightlifting unit and the table tennis club.

Liz Maxwell bravely gripped the hand of husband Fordyce as he lowered his head and wept quietly in court. Annette Hogg and Jackie Harper sat within feet of each other as the verdicts were read out. Liz praised retired post-master David Herkes whose eagle eyes had snared Black when he snatched the six-year-old in Scotland in 1990. She also said: "We have nothing but praise for the police. We couldn't have asked for more dedication. Every parent in the country can rest more easily knowing Black is in jail for the rest of his life." Sarah's gran, Marlene Hopton, kissed detective Don Naughton who had been on the case from the start and said: "Thank you."

Meanwhile, there was the question of what happened to April and Genette along with other missing girls. Suzanne Lawrence, 14, vanished as she walked home in Harold's Hill, Essex in 1969. Mystery still surrounds her disappearance. Nine-year-old Christine Markham disappeared on her way home from school in Scunthorpe, South Humberside in May 1973. Her body was never found. The body of 16-year-old trainee hairdresser Collette Aram was found partially clothed only half a mile from her home in Keyworth, Nottinghamshire in 1983. Five years later, Perrine Vigneron was found murdered in a suburb of Paris. Black's name was linked to the killing, while that same year, Virginie Delmas was the second of three girls in the French capital to be murdered. Newspapers revealed how Black could have been responsible for 15 young victims, including Patsy Morris and Dutch schoolgirl Silke Garben (10), whose body was also found in Paris, in June 1985. He was said to have been questioned about a girl in Germany, as well as over the deaths of Marion Crofts from Fleet, Hampshire, who vanished on her bike in June 1981, and Lisa Hession (14), who disappeared in December 1984 from Leigh, Greater Manchester.

The *Mirror* wrote: "One love briefly lit the bleak life of Robert Black, before he was consumed by his sickening obsession with young girls." He had even dreamed of becoming a father when he fantasized about marriage to teenage sweetheart Pamela Hodgson before she ended their relationship with a "Dear John" letter. She was his only girlfriend. He ended up having a deep distrust of women, but told police officers that his depraved criminal activities had nothing to do with his only normal relationship. For Pamela, Black had seemed "normal" at the time, and she was completely stunned by his crimes. For Black, there was to be no more love and little affection. Kids called him "Smelly Bob", and even associates described him as having "the look of a man with seedy secrets". No one, however, had an inkling he was a sex pervert wanted by six police forces in one of Britain's biggest manhunts. One expert who spent long hours probing the killer's mind believed he could have attacked hundreds of girls since his teenage days. Described as "too repulsive" to attract women, he lived for nearly 20 years in an attic flat in London, feeding on vile fantasies and a huge hoard of pornography.

As a tenant, he kept himself to himself and paid his rent

on time. He spent his evenings in his local playing snooker and darts. Outwardly, at least, he was just another beer-bellied boozer. But he had gone far beyond the schoolboy bully turned abuser. Abandoned as a baby and largely ignored ever since, he had finally found individuals he could bend to his will: small and defenceless children who wore "little girl" ankle socks. This was what drove the broad-shouldered weightlifter on his sickening quest for kicks. He had power over his victims that he had never experienced in other areas of his life. Psychiatrists believed that in his warped mind Black was wiping out memories of his own miserable childhood. Hank Williams' hit, 'Nobody's Child', was his favourite song when he was growing up. He was born to unmarried mother Jessica Black in Falkirk and was fostered at the age of six months. As a boy he lived in Kinlochleven, an Argyllshire town. Even then he had a violent streak: he didn't give a damn, according to some. No one could control him and he would never accept discipline. As a 12-year-old, Black beat up a disabled classmate in the playground for no apparent reason. According to another child at the school, Black gave the boy a "terrible hammering" and a lot of the other children were frightened of him. Black's foster parents died when he was about 14 and he flung himself into sports. He had been sent to a council children's home in Musselburgh on the outskirts of Edinburgh, where police believed he was sexually abused from the age of five by a member of staff. While Black stated he first sexually abused a child at the age of 16, police were confident that his perverted sex-driven crimes began at around the age of eight or nine, when he abducted and interfered with a neighbour's baby. He was merely admonished by a juvenile court for the air raid shelter assault on the little girl. In 1967, Black was sent to Borstal for assaulting a girl of six. After his release he moved south and landed lodgings in London. His landlords, the Rayson family, thought they were helping out another countryman; they had no idea they were inviting a callous killer to share their home. Black was thought to have kept a suitcase full of "sick souvenirs" in his flat, but police never found it. Detectives believed the locked case contained white socks stripped from his three known murder victims. While the Rayson family knew about the locked suitcase they didn't know what was in it, and by the time police turned up it had vanished. However, officers did find a massive collection of sex movies and obscene photos of Black. Kathy Rayson was horrified to discover a hoard of girls' clothes which Black kept in his room, including some of her own children's underwear. Much of the child pornography he found in London came from King's Cross. He built up a collection of magazines, including *Lollitots*, which depicted the gross sexual abuse of naked young girls.

Black kept a mattress in the back of his van, which he told associates he slept on during his long-haul deliveries. Police confirmed that one victim had lain on the mattress decomposing for two weeks before her body was dumped. He worked as a driver for Poster Despatch and Storage, and it was the petrol receipts from this company that enabled police to trace the killer's trail.

While many praised the police for the capture and conviction of Black, some questioned whether he could have been caught earlier. Vital lessons had been learned from the failings in the hunt for Peter Sutcliffe, the Yorkshire Ripper, but they didn't seem to help. Instead, it was the chance sighting by a member of the public that led to Black's downfall. The investigation that eventually led to Susan, Caroline and Sarah's killer was the largest and longest ever conducted in Britain. There were nearly 15 tons of paperwork by the end, and a specially strengthened room had to be built to house it all. Detectives were swamped by its sheer volume, which seemed to obscure the search for the perpetrator rather than leading police to him. Everything had to be added to the then new Holmes computer system (the Home Office Large Major Enquiry System) that had been set up after the chaos of the Yorkshire Ripper inquiry. It took 14 people working 14-hour days seven days a week nearly 18 months to complete the task. Police studied the cases of every child killed in the UK, Eire and the Channel Islands dating back to 1960. This research led to the creation of a unique database profiling 4,000 murders, attempted murders and other killings. The result was Catchem – Central Analytical Team Collating Homicide Expertise and Management. It was the key development in the Black investigation, and detectives hoped it would help in future cases. Yet Holmes and Catchem combined did not get to Black, even though they produced a profile of the killer in 1989. Had Black's convictions in other parts of the country been recorded on West Yorkshire files, he might have been caught sooner.

Another problem was the involvement of six police forces. On one occasion Black evaded capture when police failed to respond quickly to a 16-year-old girl who had seen him with Caroline minutes before she vanished. She described the man to police, and when she spotted him again two weeks later she immediately called the police and followed Black, but lost him in crowds. It took the police an hour to arrive. The police forces involved denied rumours that there had been rivalry between them that might have led to failings; to be fair, there were many officers who dedicated years to catching Black.

Six years after her attack, Teresa Thornhill's heart was still "gripped with hatred" as she continued to suffer from nightmares. She managed to fight free of his clutches, but the brief, shattering experience left her so traumatized that she rarely dared to leave home, because this brought on panic attacks. For Teresa, the scars remained. As she waited for the jury's verdict on the man who abducted her, she said: "Robert Black has ruined my life. I'd kill him myself. I'd be glad to. I'd give him no last rites or final requests. No mercy, no forgiveness … Then I'd pull the trigger and shoot the bastard straight between the eyes. If they brought back hanging I'd watch him drop. If he was in the electric chair, I'd push the button and watch him fry. Sorry, but he doesn't deserve to live." Teresa hadn't been able to look at Black as she gave evidence against him at Newcastle Crown Court. On 24th April 1988, on a sunny Sunday afternoon a month after her 15th birthday, Teresa had walked home alone after a trip to the park with friends. She looked closer to 10 than she did to 15. She was dressed in a pink blouse and pink skirt, and like Black's other victims she was wearing white socks. He stopped his van, turned and parked, then got out and shouted "Oi" at Teresa. She took no notice, then suddenly was seized from behind, swept off her feet and pulled tight against her abductor's belly. Black clamped his right hand over her mouth and nose, stopping her from breathing as he carried her to his van. She was too rigid with terror to react. She could smell his stale breath, and the stench of his sweat and dirt. Teresa could see the open side-door of the van and knew that he wanted to rape and kill her. But she could not have guessed the awful refinements of savagery he had in mind. Police believed that inside the van were gags, ropes and hoods and a bag of torture tools. Teresa began to fight back. As Black tried to roll her through the van door, she grabbed the bodywork and hooked her right leg underneath the sill. She sank her teeth into his forearm, making him wrench away his right hand from her mouth. She bellowed "Mum! Mum!" at the top of her voice, even though she knew her mother was nowhere near. Her friend, Andrew Beeston, whom she had left just moments before, heard her, and vaulted a fence to see

Teresa struggling in Black's arms. As he ran towards Black, Teresa grabbed Black's testicles in her freed right hand and squeezed. He bent in agony, dropping Teresa to the ground, then drove away within seconds.

Another child also suffered at the hands of Black but lived, thanks to David Herkes. The six-year-old was grabbed by the convicted killer in July 1990 as she walked along the pavement near her home in the Scottish border town of Stow. He drove off in his van towards Edinburgh, then for some reason doubled back to Stow where he had been previously spotted by Mr Herkes. When Herkes caught sight of the van for a second time, the girl's father gave chase. He found his daughter in the back of the van. He said: "I can remember David Herkes shouting: 'That's the same van. That's the same van.'" A policeman, called to the scene where the child was abducted, held up his hand but the van swerved. "I jumped in front of it and it stopped. I clambered in the back and saw a wooden partition. Up against it there was a bundle of what appeared to be rags ... When I looked closer, I saw a sleeping bag." His daughter was found inside bound, gagged and hooded. She had already been sexually assaulted. As he sat by the side of the road cradling his daughter alongside his wife, the father saw Black handcuffed at the back of the van. Mr Herkes, who had been mowing his lawn, had seen the small girl skipping down a neighbour's path before disappearing behind a blue van parked at the roadside. When she failed to reappear he immediately raised the alarm.

At Black's trial, the pain of the victim's families was evident to see. Despite the passing of time, the grief was still strong.

Two inmates at Wakefield jail in West Yorkshire appeared in court on 29th November 1995 charged with trying to murder Black. He was ambushed in his cell and attacked with scalding liquid and a table leg with a nail driven through it. The two men blinded the convicted killer with the liquid before clubbing him with the table leg, magistrates heard.

In 2002, it was hoped that DNA from Genette Tate's body might help police find her abductor. Black was mentioned again as a possible suspect, as work records showed he was in East Devon at the time of the newspaper girl's disappearance. John Tate, like the police, was convinced his daughter was dead. He said: "Before we lost Genette, I had seen reports about other missing children in the papers, but I never really gave much thought to the people and the families behind those headlines." He then described how sad life had been since his daughter's abduction. If the DNA taken from Genette's jumper is ever matched with a find on a suspect's belongings, it might bring the mystery surrounding her disappearance to an end. In April 2005 it was revealed that police would again question Black about Genette's abduction. When he was quizzed by officers, he just stared at them and refused to answer any of their questions. Originally, Black had used human rights laws to stop further interviews, but that obstacle was overcome. Black was arrested on suspicion of murdering the 13-year-old on 19th

April 2005. Police obtained Home Office permission to remove him from jail and question him at a top security police station in Leeds. On 17th May 2005, Black was arrested on suspicion of murdering a girl of nine in Northern Ireland 24 years earlier. New DNA evidence was reported to have been found in the mystery surrounding the death of Jennifer Cardy in 1981. She had been riding her new red bike, which her parents had given her for her birthday a fortnight earlier, when she was abducted, killed and dumped in a dam. Black's work records put him within a couple of miles of the crime scene. In April 2008, the *Mirror* disclosed that Black was to be charged with the girl's murder: it had taken a fresh, four-year investigation to secure enough evidence. It was, however, to be a different story for the Tate family when four months later, prosecutors said there was "insufficient evidence" to take Black to court for Genette's murder. This dealt the family a devastating blow. Genette Tate remains the subject of Britain's biggest missing persons inquiry.

Black was charged with killing Jennifer Cardy in County Antrim in December 2009. He was found guilty and convicted of her murder on 27th October 2011. Her father said the paedophile put her through an ordeal "beyond imagination". Jennifer had been going to see her best friend, but she never arrived at the post office where Louise Major lived. It took 30 years of heartache for her family to see Jennifer's killer brought to justice. Andy and Pat Cardy heard sickening details throughout the six-week trial of how Black had abducted, abused and killed their beautiful daughter. Mr Cardy said: "It has been absolutely horrendous. We heard things that, in all honesty, were not even in our imagination. We were confronted with the awfulness of her last few hours and what she had to suffer." Black snatched the nine-year-old in a quiet location in the village of Balinderry. Crucial in nailing Black was the tiny watch Jennifer was wearing when her body was found in the dam by anglers. Her mother had set it at precisely 1.40pm on the day the child vanished, the jury at Omagh Crown Court was told. It had stopped, waterlogged, at 5.40pm. This, together with garage petrol receipts, put Black in the location at the time of the little girl's disappearance. Following the conviction, Jennifer's mother said: "I don't think we will ever have closure, but we have the relief of knowing that the perpetrator of this gruesome, horrible crime has been brought to justice." She also admitted that she had missed her daughter every day for the past three decades.

Despite insufficient evidence to date, Black is still the top suspect for the murders of Genette Tate and April Fabb, as well as many other little girls. Black was given a minimum of 25 years in jail for murdering Jennifer Cardy. He is undoubtedly one of the most dangerous and criminally depraved men that Britain has ever seen. Even before this last conviction he was one of 48 UK prisoners who will never be released.

Jon Venables and Robert Thompson

(1993)

A missing toddler's body was found on a railway embankment on 14th February 1993, 48 hours after he was lured from a shopping centre by two youths. Murder squad police studied video pictures from a store's security cameras which captured the moment two-year-old James Bulger slipped away as his mother Denise queued at a butcher's in Bootle, Liverpool. The next shot showed the "beautiful bubbly boy" suddenly realizing he was lost and being "befriended" by the two youths. One frame showed blond James walking off hand in hand with one of the boys, who looked about 12 years old. Another showed frantic Denise, aged 25, searching for him. A police spokesman said: "The hunt is now on for these two youths." Four friends out playing found James' body three-and-a-half miles away and the news was broken to his parents, Ralph (26), and Denise. They had made tearful appeals for the safe return of their son. The boy's body was discovered beside the Liverpool to Kirby railway line, where a pathologist made an on the spot examination as dozens of police officers combed the track. It was thought unlikely that James could have wandered to the spot alone – as he would have had to cross at least one six-lane main road. Detectives believed the two youths might have been living rough in the area after running away from a children's home.

Police had also been informed of another sighting of the toddler with the youths about a mile from where his body was found. They were challenged by a woman and admitted they had found James, before heading off towards the railway line.

IBM experts helped police to enhance the video stills that had tracked James and the two boys. James appeared outside Alan Tym's, a butcher's shop, and police believed that he then toddled into the department store TJ Hughes and took an escalator to the floor above, emerging at Mons Square. At 3.41pm a store video camera shows the little boy looking bewildered as weekend shoppers bustled past. Then a youth, wearing a beige jacket, beckons the toddler over. In the next shot James is hand in hand with one of the two boys and heading for the exit. As they leave the centre, the two lads are in front, with James almost running to keep up a few feet behind. The last sighting of James with the boys was outside Marks & Spencer.

On 16th February 1993, the *Mirror* reported that kidnapped Jamie Bulger was battered to death with bricks – before his tiny body was sliced in two by a freight train. Sickened detectives were working on the theory that the murdered two-year-old was placed in the path of the train "for kicks". The full horror of the little boy's hideous death shocked officers "beyond words". Next to Jamie's mutilated body lay blood-stained bricks along with a bloody iron bar. His blue-hooded anorak was found hanging in a tree nearby. Superintendent Albert Kirby appealed for information on the two youths. He said: "There must be someone, somewhere, who will know their identity. They may be completely innocent. They have stupidly led the boy away. We don't know whether as a result of that he came into contact with someone else." The officer said there was no apparent motive. There was no evidence of theft or sexual abuse. Meanwhile, teams of detectives made a fingertip search of the railway track. The line was only used by two freight trains a day, heading for the docks. James Riley (14), his brother Terence (13), and their friends, David Beckett and Stephen Gunnion, both 15, found the battered body. All were said to be in a state of shock.

The police were looking for the two boys, one of whom was described as having very short dark hair and a chubby face. The second boy looked older and taller. The following day the police arrested a boy, less than two miles from where the toddler's body was found. Meanwhile, a 73-year-old woman said she saw boys with the toddler 50 minutes after he was abducted. She said: "The little one had terrific bumps on his head and the side of his face. He was screaming his head off." It was thought she was the last person, apart from his killers, to see Jamie alive. When she later saw Jamie on the television she rang police immediately, but officers thought she must have been mistaken as they believed it was too far for the toddler to walk.

Jamie had been seen by at least four witnesses being

dragged through the streets, his forehead bleeding, crying, and in a state of considerable distress. It left the community in a "pall of shame and confusion". The murder had "turned everyone's stomach".

It transpired that one mother had snatched her toddler son from the clutches of the two boys who lured Jamie to his death, when they attempted to try and get the two-year-old to walk off with them. The woman was alerted by her three-year-old daughter just one hour before Jamie went missing.

On 24th February it was revealed that the brothers and sisters of the two 10-year-olds whom police accused of murdering Jamie had been taken into care. Liverpool Social Services ensured that the siblings were given the help they needed to cope with the trauma in the aftermath of the horrific killing. Both families of the accused boys moved out of their terraced homes in the city's Walton and Norris Green areas, and the houses were boarded up to stop them being vandalized by angry mobs. Both boys who were in custody – being held in secure children's homes – were charged with Jamie's murder, and it was thought that the trial would be held as soon as possible. The committal hearing was planned for just six weeks later, and prosecutors were said to be working "flat out". Merseyside's top prosecutor Clive Woodcock said: "With juveniles of this age we do not want proceedings hanging over them."

A special dock was built in Court No. 1 at Preston Crown Court where the two boys were to appear on 1st November 1993, accused of murdering Jamie. Both boys were also charged with the attempted abduction of another two-year-old boy.

On 24th November the two boys hung their heads as Mr Justice Morland ordered for them "to be caged" for their "shocking" crime. The judge turned his anger towards horror videos – even police and lawyers were shocked by the similarities between the murder and the video *Child's Play 3*, rented by the father of one of the killers. Ordering that Robert Thompson and Jon Venables be detained for "very, very many years", the judge declared: "It isn't for me to pass judgment on their upbringing but I suspect that exposure to violent video films may in part be an explanation." It took the jury five hours and 31 minutes to return unanimous guilty verdicts on charges of murder and abduction at the end of the 17-day trial. The judge also ruled that the boys could at last be named. The accused blinked and looked bewildered as the foreman of the jury delivered the verdicts. As sentence was passed, Robert Thompson, known throughout the trial as Child A, clutched at his chest with his left hand while he took big gulps of air. Jon Venables, Child B, sat crying quietly as the judge called their crime an "act of unparalleled evil and barbarity". Passing sentence, Mr Justice Morland told the two 11-year-olds, just 10 when they murdered Jamie: "This child of two was taken from his mother on a journey of two miles and then on the railway line was battered to death without mercy, and then his body was placed across the railway line so that his body would be run over by a train in an attempt to conceal his murder. In my judgment your conduct was both cunning and very wicked." On the murder charge he sentenced the boys to be detained under secure conditions. He made no recommendation for the length of the detention, but told them they would be held until the Home Secretary was satisfied that they had matured and been rehabilitated. The judge also acknowledged that Mrs Thompson and Mr and Mrs Venables had done as much as they could to get their sons to tell the truth in police interviews.

Venables and Thompson were the youngest to serve life sentences in Britain. They joined 10 other children – the youngest of whom was 14 – who were detained indefinitely at Her Majesty's Pleasure in secure units for serious violent or sexual crimes, including murder.

Solicitor Laurence Lee, who defended Venables, said: "Certainly they will be away for a considerable amount of time. I would probably anticipate that they will not be released until they are in their mid-twenties." He told local radio that despite defending Venables he could not even begin to understand how a child so young could commit such a crime.

So what did motivate two 10-year-old boys to perpetrate such a depraved killing? *Child's Play 3*, the horrific 18-rated video mentioned at the trial, tells the story of a doll possessed by a killer. One scene shows a young boy splattered with paint being taken to a railway line. In another, the doll, which has a crazed desire to murder a child, is chopped to pieces by an air fan. The video also contains the mutilation of the young boy.

The police who questioned Venables and Thompson said: "They are evil freaks of human nature fixated on killing and causing disaster." Sergeant Phil Roberts said that Thompson had hoped to get a "buzz" from killing James and getting away with it. "The other kick was fooling the public and the police," he said. He also recalled the boy's "chilling smile" shortly after both were arrested and he saw his co-accused in the back of a police car. The sergeant continued: "I believe the smile said they knew they were responsible and thought they were going to get away with it. Venables cowered and thought other people had seen that smile." Because James' body had been mutilated by the train, another officer, PC George Scott, said: "The two boys were fixated with causing a disaster which only they would know about – which to the general public would look like an ordinary accident." Sergeant Roberts said Thompson dictated what to do, and Venable followed. He firmly believed that the boys would have killed again had they not been detected. He also stated his view that if they had got away with murder they would eventually have become "evil men".

Denise Bulger did not attend the trial of Thompson and Venables because she was expecting a baby and did not want to put her unborn child at risk. However, she was there for the verdicts, and even the tears in her eyes did not cloud her fixed concentration on her son's murderers, whom she was bravely looking at for the first time. Her eyes remained on the dock as

Thompson and Venables were sent down the 24 steps to their holding cells. When the judge wished her well with her new baby, tears began to fall for the grieving mother, and mother-to-be, who had at last seen justice done. But everyone in the courtroom knew that the family's agony would never end.

The *Mirror* reported that Thompson and Venables raced around their school playground chanting for other children to join their gang and that they were going to kill someone. Only weeks before James was dragged to his death, they challenged classmates in an appalling dare. Police interviewed fellow pupils who told them about the chanting and the "chilling call to crime". Like dozens of shocked local people, Thompson mingled with others at the murder scene where he stood among mothers and children paying their last respects to James Bulger. He even walked the 50 yards from his former home to lay a posy of picked flowers on the grassy hill beside the railway line. Police later said that both boys admitted they had avidly read newspaper reports of the killing in the days after James' death.

The *Mirror* reported: "They fitted almost every criterion for turning to crime: broken homes, learning difficulties, poor parenting, truancy and aggression. But a pitifully deprived background is no explanation for the savage murder of a two-year-old." Therapists wanted to discover why the boys killed; what motivated them and whether they could ever be returned to a normal life. They wanted to find out if they were influenced by any of the horror videos they watched, and if there were any problems in their families which left them able to switch off from the hurt and pain they were inflicting – the mark of a true psychopath. They also wanted to know if their families needed treatment – to stop them repeating whatever it was that pushed the boys into becoming killers. A top government expert said, however: "Protection of the public is more important than curing these boys. The emphasis is always on containment, not on therapy. If therapy fails, the boys face going from a secure unit to a young offenders institution, and then on to prison for the rest of their lives." If the boys were found to be psychopaths, there was no therapy.

One echo of their violence bound the two boys. Both were plagued by nightmares and both were afraid of the outside world, after vans taking them to and from court were stoned by a hate-filled mob. Venables was said not to like Thompson, blaming him and denying his own involvement. He expressed his remorse to his mother, was said to have had flashbacks to the incident and wished he could put the clock back. Meanwhile, Thompson had convinced himself that he played no part in the killing and blamed Venables entirely. There was no remorse because he didn't think he had done anything he had to be sorry for. The boys knew that they would not meet again.

It was felt that both boys had parents who cared, but they had no proper control. It was "hot-tempered" Venables, the taller of the two murderers, who was seen on video holding Jamie's hand in the shopping centre. He was also the one holding the sobbing child in a bear-hug in the street outside. He was the one who told a worried passer-by that James was his "little brother". Although Venables broke down and said he was sorry for his hideous crime when he confessed, he seemed to allude to acceptance after that, which police thought was quite unnatural. He was cold – which upset the police officers interviewing him. Venables had a strange, withdrawn nature, unable to look people in the face when he spoke to them. Both his older brother and younger sister had learning difficulties and attended special schools. Like Thompson, he was held back a year in school. His mother suffered from depression when her marriage broke up and he had been left "home alone" on occasion since the age of five. Despite this, both his parents stayed close to their children. He lived in a "poor" house in a road where others had made the break from grinding poverty. Venables was known for his explosive temper, often lashing out at other children and mimicking his wrestling heroes. He had been moved from one school to another because of his behaviour in the two years prior to James' death. Once he tried to throttle another pupil by holding a ruler to the child's larynx, and it took two teachers to restrain him. He stood on desks, he threw chairs and sometimes he rolled around the classroom walls banging his head. He was said to be jealous of the attention his older brother received and his behaviour was said to be motivated by jealousy. Despite help from social workers, Mrs Venables found it extremely difficult to control her younger son, and many of them doubted that she would carry on coping. In 1991, Venables saw a psychologist, who said he was hyperactive and suffering from a disturbed sleep pattern. When he moved schools, he found a soulmate in Thompson. At this point he began to play truant. The boys were then put in separate classes, and in the term leading up to the murder they "sagged" school four times. Of the pair, Venables was said to have caused the most trouble at school. He was described as disruptive and awkward, and was particularly difficult the day before the murder. He tended to show little emotion, but could "turn on the tears" at will. He was often fighting, but seemed to behave better under the influence of a disciplined teacher. Academically, Venables was better than average according to his former teachers, and was a lot brighter than he led people to believe. He was passed to his father by his depressive mother, and then back again when his father couldn't cope. Mrs Venables declared that her son had come from a secure and loving home, when it was suggested that he was "an urchin boy". Both Mr and Mrs Venables supported their son, despite the fact they didn't understand how he could have committed a murder, but it was clear from what they told reporters that they believed Thompson was to blame and that Venables was "weak and provoked".

"A cruel bully and a thumb-sucking crybaby" was how Thompson was known to neighbours, who also called him a "weird little bastard". He was said to have put "devil marks" on James' body according to locals, but rumours and local gossip were rife after the toddler was murdered. Thompson, the second youngest of six brothers aged between nine and 20, denied killing James when first questioned by police. His father had left his mother for a female family friend after 18 years of marriage. She was left to rear the six boys alone. (She later had another son.) Thompson, who was sometimes out until 1.00am, didn't get into serious trouble, but he became known as a sly troublemaker. He would punch and kick other kids, then try and blame others. He once tried to pull a neighbour's puppies through wire mesh so his pet polecat could bite them. He trapped birds with a fish net and he punched a little girl in the kidneys. A neighbour told reporters how Thompson was good at appearing innocent, but was really behind the "accidents" that happened – including when he let his little brother fall off a swing because he had deliberately pulled him back too far. He was academically slow at school and did not mix well with other children. Of Thompson and Venables, Thompson, according to teachers, was the dominant one. He was often cruel to his younger brother, but his mother protested her son's innocence to the bitter end. She blamed his school, social workers, neighbours and the police for failing to keep a track on him. When asked about her son's future, she said: "If I knew that I would be a bloody psychologist." Asked where it would all end for him, she replied: "In a coffin."

When together, the worst aspects of both boys' characters

combined, to end in killing. The police confirmed that in their belief the boys set out to kill that fateful day. They still did not understand why – but what they did know was that the boys seemed to have an unspoken understanding. Superintendent Kirby said: "I truly believe they are just evil and there is nothing to provide any excuse for them. They are two boys with bad intent who came together and created a terrible evil." Both mothers – who had tried to find an explanation for their sons' murderous intent – believed that the "other boy" had spurred them on, and the mothers blamed each other.

During the attack on James his lower clothing was removed and his wet underpants draped on his head. One of his attackers had been a bed-wetter: was the same "punishment" meted out to him? There was slight, irregular damage to James' genitals. Did that mean something? By themselves, the findings did not constitute sufficient evidence to suggest that a sex attack had taken place, but experts shared a strong belief that there was a sexual motive. In a study of sexual homicide, the FBI examined which children grow up to be sex-killers, and concluded that they were from broken homes and endured a poor relationship with their mothers: "Murderers describe themselves as shy or loners. Instead they retreat into their own sexually violent fantasy worlds." It is a private world of violence over which they can exercise control. They daydream, they lie, they wet the bed, rebel, have nightmares, destroy property, are cruel to other children and to animals. They play truant throughout their school years, although many are above average intelligence. Forensic clinical psychologist David Glasgow of Liverpool University firmly believed in the link with "chemistry". He said: "Children who are isolated and actively avoided by their peers are very vulnerable to developing this sort of behaviour. If you get two who click together, they feed off each other." He added his own belief that sexual gratification – for one of the boys at least – formed part of the murder.

The Bulger family and the public in general were outraged in January 1994 when it transpired that Mr Justice Moreland, despite what he had said at the trial, had recommended to the Home Secretary that the boys serve a minimum of eight years. Thompson still hadn't acknowledged his guilt. More than 75,000 TV viewers backed the Bulgers' campaign to keep the killers in prison for all their lives. Ralph and Denise Bulger launched the nationwide petition after it was revealed that the judge had recommended eight-year sentences. Home Secretary Michael Howard, in contrast, wanted the boys to serve a minimum of 15 years, but this was quashed by the High Court in May 1996 when it ruled that his decision was "unlawful".

Fury hit the headlines again in March 1999, when it was announced that the boys were appealing. Denise Fergus – James' mother had by now remarried – "attacked" the decision to refer the killers' case to the European Court of Human Rights. The boys, by now 16, were challenging their convictions and sentences, having had their eight-year sentences increased to 15. Lawyers claimed they were not treated fairly because they were tried in an adult court. The Bulger family believed that this was a technicality but Paul Cavadino, of the National Association for the Care and Resettlement of Offenders, said: "Almost everywhere else in Europe these boys would be dealt with by family courts concerned with the need for compulsory measures of care." For the family, however, it was an insult to James. On what should have been the murdered toddler's ninth birthday, that same month, Denise was left trying to come to terms with a European judgment that said her son's killers did not get a fair trial for his brutal murder. She said: "Those two boys are evil and they knew what they were doing. This legal wrangling is disgusting. It was a premeditated crime and they were fully responsible for the most horrible murder." Whatever the outcome of the appeal, Britain could not be forced to release the pair. When it transpired in 2000 that the boys could possibly avoid an adult prison, the murdered toddler's family was furious. According to reports, the murderers were to be spared prison when they legally became adults at the age of 18. Instead, they could be ordered to stay in secure council care until they turned 19, but they could avoid jail altogether if they were released before this. Denise said: "They are not boys any more and it is time they paid for what they did. To this day they have had no real punishment for murdering James. They have only had the best care and attention and a fine education. If they get more of the soft life it sends a message to other children that there is no punishment for the most horrific crimes. If they are let out at 19 it means they will get away with murder." Thompson's lawyer, Dominic Lloyd, argued that the boys were being treated the same as "anyone else", and that meant being transferred between the ages of 18 and 19 and not going to an adult prison until the age of 21.

In November 2000 Venables and Thompson went to court to "demand a new life of freedom in secret". The pair asked a judge to keep a ban on publicity about them for the rest of their lives – the *Mirror* and other newspapers opposed these plans. The court hearing came after Lord Chief Justice Lord Woolf said their term should end. A Parole Board hearing in early 2001 was expected to set them free. They would then be given new identities and new lives away from the scene of their crime. An injunction granted in July 2000 had banned the media from talking about or publishing photos of the boys, or reporting their progress or treatment. In a "unique" and unprecedented move, Dame Elizabeth Butler-Sloss, President of the High Court Family Division, was asked to make it permanent. She ruled in early 2001 that they would be able to keep their identities secret and she banned the publication of information that could identify them. She said: "I am compelled to take steps to protect their lives. These young men are uniquely notorious and are at risk of attacks from members of the public as well as from relatives and friends of the murdered child." Ralph Bulger had repeatedly said he was prepared to do everything he could to track Venables and Thompson down if they were ever set free. Dame Butler-Sloss ordered that they should be granted anonymity for the rest of their lives, ruling that their new names, appearances and addresses could never be revealed. She said: "Threats to injure and kill them have been set out in the evidence presented to me. There remains among some members of the public a serious desire for revenge if the two young men are living in the community. The Home Office views these threats seriously and is likely to give Venables and Thompson new identities on their release. I am convinced that their lives are genuinely at risk …" The only other child murderer to convince the Home Office that she was at significant risk was Mary Bell in 1960. The crime reduction charity Nacro welcomed the High Court ruling, and Harry Fletcher of the National Association of Probation Officers said: "The authorities in the secure unit where they have been held have come to a decision that they no longer present a risk to the public." The decision was also welcomed by Unlock, the national association of ex-offenders. The injunction only applied in England and Wales, however, so there were concerns that the internet or foreign media could be used to track down the murderers' new identities.

In February 2001, two lawyers were said to have clashed bitterly in the High Court over claims that Thompson had beaten up two boys in the secure unit. He allegedly had a dispute with killer John Howells (16), over "who had committed the most evil crime". He was also alleged to have attempted to strangle

Scott Walker. However, David Pannick, QC, representing Home Secretary Jack Straw, said the story in the *Sunday People* had been invented. In June 2001, Mothers Against Murder staged a protest outside the Parole Board's HQ in London as the board was expected to decide if Venables and Thompson no longer posed a risk and if they should order their release "on licence". In July 2001, it was reported that "Bulger Killers Are Out", and living in halfway houses under 24-hour supervision. First, they took a week-long holiday, which a source said "was to get them away during the initial uproar over the decision to free them". Both youths had new identities backed up by false birth certificates.

For nine years there was very little, if no, mention of Venables and Thompson in the media. However, in March 2010 it was reported that Venables was back behind bars at the age of 27 because he broke the conditions set when he was released in 2001. The dramatic recall was revealed by the Ministry of Justice, which was contacted by the *Mirror*. Criminal law expert Michael Wolkind, QC, said he thought there was a "significant chance" the breach had been serious. The *Mirror* reported that Venables' life had descended into one of drug abuse and brushes with the law since he left jail, and that he began snorting cocaine and popping ecstasy pills while throwing himself into his local nightclub scene. He was also said to have a raging temper that had landed him in a lot of trouble with the police, and he was finally hauled back to prison after a bust-up at work. He had been arrested by police on suspicion of affray outside a nightclub, after an angry boyfriend of a girl who was at the club punched Venables in the face. He was released without charge, but at work he was said to have "flipped without warning". He grappled with the other person before others intervened and pulled them apart. His alleged victim was said to have made an official complaint about the attack. Venables was suspended from work and subjected to an "immediate" recall to jail. He was, at this time, working for the minimum wage, living in a bedsit in the north of England. A source then lifted the lid on Venables' secret life of drug addiction: up until Christmas 2009 he had been buying a gram of cocaine a week to feed his habit. Meanwhile, ministers faced growing anger over their refusal to explain why he had been returned to prison, but a Justice Ministry spokesman said: "We can confirm that Jon Venables has been recalled to custody following a breach of licence conditions. Offenders on licence are subject to strict conditions …" Venables should not have returned to Merseyside under these strict conditions, but it was revealed that "skulking into Liverpool under his new identity … Jon Venables cynically flouted his strict parole rules to go on wild benders with mates". In a cruel snub to the memory of James, he had been frequenting nightclubs in the city to get smashed on cider and cocktails while taking cocaine and ecstasy. Sources revealed that he also slipped into Goodison Park to watch Everton play during the nine years he had been free, and had chatted up women in clubs and pubs not far from where he and Thompson had battered James to death. He was also said to have snorted kitty, a legal drug also known as methadone, miaow or MCAT, while downing Cheeky Vimtos, a cocktail of two shorts of port and a bottle of blue WKD. He was spotted in Krazy House, The Funky Box, Bar Fly and Walkabout on more than one occasion. He also visited the Cavern Club and watched the band Keane at the Liverpool Arena. In fact, one source said he tried to stay in Liverpool for as long as possible, but had never returned to Bootle, the district where he had snatched James. This was daring behaviour for a man living under a new identity, in a city where he was probably more at risk than in any other should anyone realize who he was.

Just a few days after the news that Venables was back behind bars, the real reason for his "immediate recall" was revealed. It was alleged that he had committed a serious sex offence that could keep him behind bars for at least two years: the *Sunday Mirror* reported that he was facing child porn allegations. Ralph Bulger said: "Once evil, always evil and I have never felt any differently about Venables or Thompson. They will never care how much they hurt people and destroy lives. I am sickened to the stomach to hear Venables is back in jail for an alleged sex offence. If he's guilty, I'm horrified to think another family faces a lifetime of torture because he was free to hurt more innocent victims. But I can't say that I am surprised. This is why we never wanted either of these twisted killers released in the first place." The allegations were said to be "extremely serious", and reports also suggested that Venables himself had been revealing his true identity.

The social worker who spent eight years looking after Thompson at the detention centre where he was held said he never showed any remorse for James' murder. He said the child-killer was unemotional and detached, taking his conviction "in his stride". He added: "He was monosyllabic and sullen when we were first introduced. But it became apparent he was what we call a typical 'care kid' – even though he hadn't been in care. These children are cocky and streetwise, know the system and what they can get away with." He said that Thompson was "obsessed" with news reports of his trial, was regularly visited and "fussed over" by Home Office officials and treated with "kid gloves" by centre staff, who feared that "something might happen to him". The social worker said Thompson wasn't a troublemaker, but would stand up for himself if he had to. The social worker added: "There was plenty of pure evil in his unit. But if you didn't know who killed James and had to pick the killer from the offenders, Robert would have been the last person. He had a good sense of humour and picked up on staff jokes that the rest of the kids wouldn't get. He was very bright. I can't see Robert going the same way as Venables. He is just too smart. He will hate what has happened because it will once more put his name in the spotlight."

Meanwhile, the row about why Venables was in jail raged

on. Denise Fergus rounded on Justice Secretary Jack Straw for refusing to say what the reason was, claiming that by keeping it secret he was "protecting a criminal". On 11th March 2010, the *Mirror* said: "Jon Venables had nine explosive outbreaks of violent temper shortly before experts declared he posed a 'trivial' risk to the public and could be freed." The psychiatric report on the killer recorded all the incidents of his bad behaviour in one year. But the assessment insisted that the chance of him reoffending was "so negligible as to not amount to a serious consideration". The report, prepared in August 2000 but not made public for nearly nine years, said: "immediate release would be justified".

A jury member in the James Bulger trial slammed the early release of Venables. Alan Barry said: "If Venables is guilty of new offences he should be locked up for a very long time. I can still see the photos of the injuries we had to look at, which were horrendous. It is still so vivid." He added: "They should have been sentenced to a lot longer in prison. I, and other jurors, were surprised at what they got. Although they were only 10 I believe they knew what they were doing. A sentence like that was ludicrous." Retired Detective Sergeant Phil Roberts said he thought that neither killer was capable of rehabilitation.

Once Venables' identity was revealed in the prison (which couldn't be named) where he was being held, prison officers put an astonishing regime in place to stop other inmates getting to him, and the Prison Service went to extraordinary lengths to keep his presence secret. He was moved to a new high security jail in the days just before 15th March, a significant distance from where he had been held previously, amid fears he was in serious danger from prisoners who had learned who he was. He was then kept in strict isolation in a sealed unit, where he was monitored by CCTV 24 hours a day. A hand-picked team was said to be guarding him. They referred to him only by his prison number and were ordered not to identify him. The newspapers reported that Venables could spend up to five years in prison – even if he managed to dodge criminal charges. The Ministry of Justice denied a report that a decision had been taken not to prosecute him, but even if he did escape a trial, he still had to attend a Parole Board hearing, where officials had the power to lock him up for years. If so, he would start serving any sentence immediately.

The new jail was said to be a significant distance from where he was held previously amid new allegations against him. The age of criminal responsibility in England was one of the youngest in Europe (age 10). It was seven in Switzerland, Nigeria and South Africa, but eight in Scotland. In France it was 14 and in Germany, Bulgaria, Romania and China it was 15. The oldest age of criminal responsibility existed in Belgium and Luxembourg, at 18. In other parts of the world, it was 10 in Australia and New Zealand and 18 in most of the United States.

Denise Fergus called for the Children's Commissioner, Dr Maggie Atkinson, to be sacked for dismissing her son's murder as "unpleasant" in March 2010. She also wanted an apology for what she called "twisted and insensitive comments". The Children's Commissioner had said that the killers should not have been prosecuted at such a young age because they were not old enough to know the "full consequences" of their actions, and that "what they did was exceptionally unpleasant". Mrs Fergus said that to call what the murderers did "unpleasant" was outrageous. She argued that although the Commissioner's job was to stand up for children, what about James? With regard to the Commissioner's comments that the killers should have had "programmes" to turn their lives around and that they should not have been jailed, Denise said: "This woman should get her facts right. They never spent a day in jail. They were sent to children's homes where they had kid-glove treatment, computer games and the best of everything." She added: "They were rewarded for murder and left thinking they got away with it. The fact that Venables has been accused of breaching his parole shows that all the programmes he was put on did not change him."

The row was further fuelled by Children's Secretary Ed Balls who claimed that Venables and his accomplice were not "intrinsically evil". Speaking at a press conference in Westminster, Balls insisted youngsters deserved a second chance, no matter what they had done. He said: "I think you have to be very careful to ever label a child as 'intrinsically evil'. Children are very affected by what happened to them when they are growing up. I personally believe in rehabilitation and change." His remarks put him at odds with Mrs Fergus, who urged officials to recognize Venables and Thompson as "evil".

In a further snub to James' family, the arrogant Venables was acting in jail as if he was untouchable, claiming that he would soon be freed. He rejected treatment with a sex offenders' programme, sneering that he wouldn't be inside long enough to complete it. He defied threats by inmates and was known to be receiving preferential treatment to foil revenge attacks. He bragged: "I can take all the abuse." Sources told the *Mirror*: "Venables is now walking around his new prison as if he owns the place." He was said to be associating with drug dealers and users on his wing, but refusing to co-operate with jail bosses' repeated requests for voluntary drug-testing and educational courses. He told one officer: "I don't want any courses that take long as I'll be out sooner rather than later." One source said: "He has an inflated sense of his own importance. He thinks he's better than other lags and ignores all advice to keep his head down. And he refused to take part in anger management and sex offender courses, even though they've been identified as crucial to his rehabilitation." The source said Venables received several threats after being recognized but refused to back down. "He is with drug culture people most of the time, instead of keeping a low profile as he was advised. But it may be to protect himself from attacks. Venables did say one inmate recognized him from his previous time behind bars.

He tells other prisoners he can handle all the abuse and threats because he's used to it and he hasn't reported any problems to staff."

The Children's Commissioner told Radio 4's *Woman's Hour*: "There's a private letter of apology from me going to her [Mrs Fergus] for the hurt caused." Her earlier remarks had caused a great deal of anger, but the Commissioner tried to calm the furore, saying she had not intended to make a "call of any sort".

Despite his cockiness, it was announced in April 2010 that Venables faced a six-month wait in jail owing to a backlog of cases. He was the subject of a police investigation, and sources said that any court case would take precedence over a review of his parole. Meanwhile, Jack Straw pledged to keep Denise Fergus informed of all developments.

It transpired later that month that Venables turned himself in to jail after admitting he was revealing his true identity to strangers. He allegedly began bragging in pubs and online that he was the killer of James Bulger, putting himself at serious risk of reprisals. Probation officers were said to be furious at his actions because it meant he would need a new identity, costing tens of thousands of pounds. Venables told officials he was in a disturbed emotional state, sparking an inquiry into his behaviour. During the probe it was found he had allegedly downloaded child porn, so he was hauled back to jail and had to prove that he could live under another false name before having any chance of parole. Retraining for his new identity could, it was claimed, take six months. An insider said: "Staff are going to drill him like a raw recruit to the Army until he knows his story backwards. Then he will be drilled again until he knows that mouthing off about his past will land him in serious trouble. They can't go through this whole process a third time, it would be ridiculous, so Venables will not be released until they're happy he won't jeopardize his position again." One probation worker added: "Venables is in the last chance saloon, he was given unprecedented support and a new identity at huge public cost. We can't afford to have him mess up again otherwise the system becomes a farce." At this point, Venables denied the indecent images found by police on his computer were downloaded by him. He was sharing a house, and unless officers could prove nobody else had access to the laptop he would not be prosecuted. If no charges were brought, Venables would have to apply for parole at a hearing, but any release would be delayed for many months while he was given a stack of new personal data.

Harry Fletcher, of probation union Napo, said: "Jon Venables should not be released unless the Parole Board believe his risk of reoffending is low and he will comply with the terms of his licence ..." But in June 2010 it was reported that he faced charges of downloading 57 child porn images. The accusations against him were revealed for the first time after an Old Bailey judge lifted a legal gag on reporting the case. Venables was claimed to have stored the indecent video clips and pictures on his computer. He was also charged with distributing seven images of children under 11 by allowing other web users to access his computer files. Denise Fergus said: "It is right the charges he faces should be made public."

She praised the judge who agreed to make public the child porn charges, and said: "I simply want to see justice done." She added: "I have been kept informed, to an extent, about the legal proceedings in the case over the past few months, through the Ministry of Justice, the Merseyside Probation Service and, more recently, senior officers from Merseyside Police. My solicitor has also been in touch with the Ministry of Justice, to make representations on my behalf and to raise a number of concerns I have about the way the case is to be handled. We are still awaiting a reply to that formal approach. I don't want to say anything that could affect the proceedings. I'm prepared to wait and see what happens." But a solicitor for Ralph Bulger said the Ministry of Justice had blundered by trying to throw a blanket of secrecy around the Venables case since it was revealed he had been returned to prison. Robin Makin, speaking outside the Old Bailey after Mr Justice Bean lifted the legal gag on reporting the specific charges, added: "We consider that the way this has been handled … has been a disaster. The public authorities ought to behave quite differently and, in due course, further details are likely to emerge of mistakes made. Ineptitude and incompetence spring to mind." Venables was not in court as the gag was lifted and was due to face a plea and case management hearing on 23rd July 2010, when he would appear at the Old Bailey using a videolink from prison. Media law expert Mark Stephens said that Venables would get a fair hearing despite the publicity surrounding the case: "The judge has gone to extraordinary lengths, as has the prosecution, to make sure a fair trial can happen."

However, Denise Fergus "slammed the cover-up" investigation that had allowed the killer to reoffend. A report admitted there had been a string of failings, but concluded the probation service couldn't have known Venables was spiralling out of control after he was freed from his secure unit in 2001. Mrs Fergus said: "Venables is devious, cunning and dangerous. He cannot be trusted and that is what they need to remember." She said the report was a "classic cover-up" and that Justice Secretary Ken Clarke had betrayed her. Sir David Omand's report said the killer might not have reoffended if he had got a better job and been given more therapy; and that probation staff had got too close to him to spot the dangers. Mr Clarke said the report found that "reasonable supervision" could not have stopped Venables from offending again. Venables admitted to the charges of child pornography in July 2010 at the Old Bailey, and was given a two-year sentence.

It then emerged in March 2011 that at the age of 17, before his release, Venables had had an affair with a woman who worked in the secure children's unit. Denise Fergus immediately called for an inquiry. The woman who had sex with Venables was accused of sexual misconduct, suspended and did not return to her job. Mrs Fergus wanted to know if information was withheld from Lord Chief Justice Woolf when he made Venables and Thompson eligible for parole in 2000. At the time, he referred to reports that said they had made excellent progress. Mrs Fergus said: "I sat in the court in October 2000 and heard Lord Woolf saying he had been handed glowing reports on them. The main reason he gave for allowing them to be released early was their supposed good behaviour. But now we know that was not the truth and it is clear that the reports sent to Lord Woolf were rubbish. I want a full inquiry about how false reports were given to the judges. The woman should have been prosecuted and if not, why? I was told at the time they were like holiday camps behind bars and that evil pair had not been rehabilitated."

The Red Bank Community Home in Merseyside was a separate unit at a former borstal, which was designed to get inmates used to living a "normal life" prior to release. Two years before Venables had sex with the woman carer, a guard at the children's unit was disciplined for getting "too close" to an inmate. Venables was there at the time, but it was not known if he was the child in question. Papers relating to the 1998 incident, revealed under Freedom of Information laws, have since been destroyed in accordance with local council policy. The revelations added fuel to the demands for a public inquiry. Meanwhile, the woman carer wasn't prosecuted and officials refused to comment.

Exactly 16 years to the day he murdered James Bulger, Venables had a raucous night out to celebrate a friend's birthday, during which he was reported to have drunk heavily. The publication of a photograph of this occasion online, showing Venables grinning, sparked fury. Despite a gagging order, meaning that newspapers could not publish the image or disclose the website it was on, more than 1,500 people viewed it.

Venables was also rumoured to be going back in front of the Parole Board, meaning that he might only serve half his two-year sentence for child pornography. Ralph Bulger said: "The only fitting punishment for him is life imprisonment. I urge the Parole Board to not just consider his latest crimes against children but to look at the whole picture, which is that he is a murdering, predatory paedophile who poses an immediate risk to young children. Nothing I do can ever bring James back but I will fight to my dying breath to protect my other children and any other youngster from ever being a victim of Jon Venables again." Denise Fergus stated that the killer's identity should no longer be protected. She branded the gagging order as "ridiculous", and said that Venables was a criminal and not part of a witness protection programme. It was alleged at the time that Venables' personal details were being passed around online, and in November 2011 it was reported that he could remain behind bars for life because he could not keep his new identity secret, and was repeatedly blabbing his name, something he continued to do, raising the risk of revenge attacks, so jail chiefs refused to release him. Denise Fergus was delighted by the news and accused the killer of seeing himself as a "celebrity" who got a "thrill" from telling people who he was. At the time, the papers reported that he wouldn't be given a new name because he could not be trusted to blurt it out. A prison source was quoted as saying: "If he was given a new identity, chances are he'd compromise it. That puts him in danger of vigilante attacks. It is safer for him if he remains in custody. He got a life sentence for the murder of James Bulger, so they can keep him as long as they want." Another source said: "It would be a waste of money giving him a new identity because he can't keep his real name secret." Denise said: "In his twisted mind he believes the name Jon Venables makes him some kind of celebrity. He can't resist telling people who he is. He gets some kind of perverse thrill from it and it's clear therefore that he has no remorse about murdering my son. It all shows he cannot be trusted and shouldn't be paroled."

David Wilson, Professor of Criminology at Birmingham University, wrote: "Venables found living with an assumed identity difficult. He would get drunk, get high and say who he was. So, I doubt he would be able to live with a new assumed identity without at some stage revealing that too. Prison is a much more structured environment where you can segregate people for their own safety. If I was on the Parole Board I'd think about the fact that he was still fighting, using cocaine and downloading child pornography after all the work that had been done. I'd need to be satisfied that had all been dealt with before I would consider parole."

In an exclusive interview in February 2013 with Luke Traynor, solicitor Laurence Lee described what happened when he met his client, Jon Venables, in 1993. He thought there must have been a terrible mistake as he peered down at the young lad at the police station. Laurence did not believe his new client – a boy aged 10 – could have been involved in the brutal crime that officers were accusing him of. He was accustomed to dealing with appalling offences but nothing could prepare him for the catalogue of evil to which young Jon Venables would confess. Speaking to Traynor just a few days before the 20th anniversary of James' murder, he described how the "chilling memories of the sickening case" were still etched on his mind. In particular, he would never forget the detached and cold attitude of 10-year-old killer Thompson. Recalling the first moment he saw his client, Laurence said: "I went to Lower Lane police station and he was sat with his mother, Sue, a respectable lady. I couldn't believe this small boy was involved in this crime. He looked almost angelic. When the officer interviewed Venables, he said he'd been nowhere near the Strand shopping centre, and I thought I had been brought along under false pretences. It was only when the officers compared notes with what Robert Thompson was saying in his interviews at Walton police station that it didn't add up.

"Venables kept up his denials, then suddenly there was silence before he wailed, 'OK, we did go to the Strand, but I never grabbed a kid'. There was wailing, and the walls caved in. He was hugging his mum, grabbing officers. I wanted to stop the interview as he was getting tired and his mother was distressed. As I left the station I had to check under my car for explosives in case of reprisals. I was a security target as I was representing Venables."

The following day, Venables admitted his gruesome crimes and Laurence said: "What we heard reached the depths of depravity. And Venables said, 'We did kill James – please tell his mum we're sorry.'" After coaxing James for two miles to Walton, the boys attacked James on the railway line. Paint was splashed in his eyes before the pair stamped on him. James had 10 skull fractures – and a total of 42 injuries. Bricks and stones were hurled at the toddler during a degrading assault. A 22lb iron bar was dropped on him before Thompson and Venables laid their victim's body across the railway line to try to cover up his murder as an accident. Two days later, his body was found severed by the impact from a freight train. Laurence said that Thompson was the instigator, but the lawyer dismissed Venables' claims about playing a minor role. Sitting in his wife's café in Liverpool, he added: "Venables was a conniving little liar, although he showed a lot more emotion than Thompson ever did. Thompson was the coldest child I've ever seen. Venables said he'd thrown stones at James, but missed on purpose. He claimed Thompson picked up on this, and shouted, 'Are you blind, divvy?'

"That was Venables' defence. That Thompson had been the driving force. But he was far more involved in the attack than he wanted us to believe. During those interviews, his parents were shell-shocked and Venables was crying. We also walked along the route they took James, which was a horrible experience for everybody."

The father of three only spoke with Thompson once – but it left an indelible mark. "I first saw Thompson at the ID parade. I put my head against the glass and he said to me, 'You're a fucking ugly bastard.' That's the type of boy he was."

Riots had erupted outside Sefton Magistrates' Court in Merseyside in February 1993 as Thompson and Venables made their first appearance in court. Laurence said: "At court Thompson sat twiddling the ring on his finger. Venables listened but it was all over his head. We got the dock raised by 18 inches so the boys could see over the top. It was a landmark case in many ways. Thompson's mum screamed after the case, 'He may be a fucking robber, but he's not a murderer.'" Laurence described how Venables reoffending came as a shock to him. He thought it was much more likely that Thompson would "transgress again". Referring to Venables' application for parole in the summer of 2013, Laurence said: "I couldn't believe Venables was trying for release on the back of the 20th anniversary of James' death. It's horribly timed. If Venables is trying to claw back sympathy, he's going about it the wrong way." He added: "The case 20 years ago really affected me. At the end of the trial I had terrible flashbacks and nightmares. It took me months to get back to any sort of normality."

As a result of Venables' bid for freedom, Denise Fergus was set to make an emotional personal appeal to Parole Board chiefs in February 2013. She firmly believed he was still a danger to the public. Speaking on the night before the anniversary of her son's death, Mrs Fergus said she believed Venables was a psychopath who had shown a disturbing pattern of sexual deviancy. She pointed to his conviction for downloading child porn as evidence that he had not reformed. Venables had also posed online as a woman of 35, pretending to have an eight-year-old daughter available for rent to paedophiles. Denise said: "My message to the Parole Board is don't release Jon Venables. People say kids aren't born evil. But I strongly believe he was. On that computer, he had images of kids being abused as young as two. He's still a danger to the public. He's blown his second chance. The images were disgusting. I believe he could go on to do another serious crime.

"There are indications Venables is an undiagnosed psychopath. He's being kept in a prison when he should have been transferred to a secure hospital. He's not right in the head. To kill a kid, to have all these things on his PC. I'm not saying he should never be released … But now is not the right time because he is a danger." Denise was said to be angry at the legal protocol which would allow Venables to read her personal statement before it was recounted to the Parole Board, although she was unable to see his version of how he believed he had been rehabilitated. She said: "It's all one-sided." Her lawyer, Sean Sexton, had asked for assurances that the board would see evidence that James' murder was sexually motivated before they gave their ruling. Asked if she would consider meeting her son's killers, Denise said: "I wouldn't get the truth out of them. They are cunning liars. I've still got anger and hatred towards Thompson and Venables. I'll never forgive them."

In a move that was slammed by Denise as a dangerous "gamble", Venables was granted parole in July 2013. She was said to be stunned at the news which she received by telephone on 4th July, especially as she had been told by the Parole Board six weeks earlier that there would be a full investigation of a dossier of "inconvenient truths", which she said had been swept under the carpet. One of these was the indication that there was a sexual motive to James' murder. Lawyers for Ralph Bulger said: "The living nightmare continues and is exacerbated by this reckless decision. It fills Ralph with terror." Conditions of the parole were not known at the time, but a spokesman said: "He will be released. All parties were told."

Venables was secretly released from jail in the summer of 2013 and given a fourth assumed identity. Denise, who was given the news on 2nd September, said: "He lies for his own sick ends. I have been told that the terms of his parole mean that he must not enter the county of Merseyside. But the probation service didn't monitor him properly last time so I have no faith in their ability to do that now." It had taken two months for officials to prepare the murderer for release. Ralph Bulger demanded that the freed Venables be sent as far away from his family as possible. He feared the 31-year-old still posed a danger, and believed that the only way his family would be safe was if the "pervert is ordered to live in the South" and told to stay away from Liverpool. Ralph was adamant that the killer would breach the conditions of his release banning him from Merseyside if he was allowed to live in the North West. His solicitor, Robin Makin, said: "Ralph has suggested he should be far away from Merseyside, but we don't know if the authorities are listening to us. Ralph believes there will be problems in the future with Venables. Neither his family or the public are protected from this man. Venables should be at the opposite end of the country." Denise called for an overhaul of the parole system after the controversial release. She claimed officials failed to inform her of conditions of the paedophile's licence before he was freed. She said: "I believe he's fooled the Parole Board." With Venables freed, the nightmare continues for James Bulger's family.

Ian Huntley

(2002)

On Monday 5th August 2002, 500 volunteers joined a desperate search for two missing 10-year-old girls wearing David Beckham replica shirts. Police and the parents of best friends Holly Wells and Jessica Chapman urged the girls to "phone home". Detectives were "extremely concerned" by the disappearance of the pair the night after a barbecue at Holly's home. The girls were said to be happy, intelligent children who had never gone missing before. It was thought that they had no money and no change of clothes. Detectives had hoped to trace them via Jessica's mobile phone, but there was no reply and it went dead at 1.30am on 5th August. Officers promptly arranged for it to be "topped up" in case credit had run out. The girls' distraught parents, from the Cambridgeshire market town of Soham, made an emotional appeal to them and assured them they would not be in trouble. Jessica's father, Leslie Chapman (51), told a news conference: "All is forgiven, just come home … Jessica is bright and intelligent. She knows to use the phone and it is a complete mystery why she has not phoned. It is out of character." Her mother, Sharon (42), a learning support assistant at the girls' school, said Jessica wasn't streetwise, but she wasn't stupid either. Holly's dad, Kevin Wells (38), said: "They were fine when they were playing here. We think they must have gone out for sweets." He didn't think Holly, a majorette who played the cornet, would be too frightened to come home. He said: "They are very bright girls and I would say to them: 'Don't think for a moment you are going to be told off.'" He added: "We are really worried something untoward has happened."

Mr Wells described his daughter as a "fantastic girl". Jessica had not long returned home from a holiday in Minorca. On 4th August she went to Holly's house, just around the corner, to give her a present she had brought back. They played on Holly's computer, then visited a sports centre before having something to eat at about 5.30pm. Then they went upstairs to play, before going missing about an hour later. The classmates were last spotted by a member of the public a few hundred metres from Holly's home at 6.30pm, walking along Sand Street towards the town centre in their red Manchester United shirts with "David Beckham" and his team number 7 on the back. Two hours later, the barbecue at the Wells' family home came to an end. Holly's mother, Nicola (35), said: "Our friends went to leave at about 8.30pm and we mentioned how quiet the girls had been. When we went to check on them, they had gone." The two sets of parents launched their own hunt before calling police. They searched from Wickham to Soham, where they tracked a mobile signal from one of the girls' phones, but it went dead. When the police were informed, volunteers – all local residents – gathered in Soham to join police search teams. A helicopter and dogs were brought in.

Once police were involved they checked the sex offenders' register for a possible abduction suspect, then examined Holly's computer to see if the girls had been using the internet and gone to meet someone they had met online. Along with their Manchester United shirts, both girls were wearing dark trousers and Nike trainers.

The hunt for the two children began again at dawn and a police helicopter joined police and civilian volunteers. At 9.00am the police issued an appeal, and told the public that they were "increasingly concerned". Later in the day the girls' parents appeared at a press conference to appeal for help. One woman came forward, believing that she had seen the girls walking on the path outside her home in Little Thetford – eight miles away from where they vanished – more than 12 hours after they went missing. This gave fresh hope to four anguished parents. Another woman claimed to have seen the girls later the same day walking along the busy A10 that heads towards Cambridge. Fighting back tears, Nicola Wells said: "The sighting has given us a bit of hope. We hope it's them and they are OK and will find their way back." Her husband Kevin added: "We really would welcome a snippet that would lead us to finding Holly and Jessica. The sighting has been a fantastic response to the appeal and it has given us an extra glimmer of hope." He described how family and friends had been searching ditches and rivers, looking for shallow graves. "It doesn't get any more difficult than that" he continued. Superintendent David Hankins said: "The sighting gives us hope and it means the children were happy, not distressed. You can never be 100 per cent sure but the description matches the girls to a T. If it was them, someone else must have seen them. The road would have been quite busy and I am surprised we have not had any more sightings. If the two girls were not Jessica and Holly then I would urge them to come forward so that we can rule out that line of inquiry and not waste time. What is baffling is we need a motive as to why they left home. They don't appear to have planned it."

The police search was widened. Bloodhounds were brought in and specialist divers searched the many rivers and ponds in the fens that surround Soham. Police also took away both families' computers to try to discover why the girls disappeared. They were said to have enjoyed sending emails and police wanted to know if they had arranged to meet anyone, although both sets of parents were sure that their daughters didn't know enough about the internet and chatrooms in particular to have met someone online. Experts also checked Jessica's phone records. Superintendent Hankins said: "This is one of the largest missing persons investigations that this force has ever conducted. There are more than 100 officers working on the investigation. Many of them are parents." He urged people to search sheds, outbuildings and abandoned cars. "We live in hope, but the longer they are away from their parents, the greater the risk and the anxiety," he said. Diane Wesley,

Holly's grandmother, said: "All I can think is that someone has picked them up and taken them off somewhere. But how do you take two children? It's just impossible to think you could take two of them ... what has happened is just devastating." Detective Superintendent Alan Ladley, who led the hunt for the killer of schoolgirl Sarah Payne, was brought in to help with the investigation. He and Detective Inspector Martyn Underhill had arrested known paedophile Roy Whiting, who was later jailed for life for murdering eight-year-old Sarah. Meanwhile, another senior police source said: "We have been treating this as a missing persons inquiry rather than an abduction but it is building up to the latter. With these officers arriving I think it will be seen that this is the way the inquiry is going."

David Beckham made a personal appeal to Jessica and Holly to go home in a statement issued jointly with his Manchester United teammates. He said: "Please go home. You are not in any kind of trouble. Your parents love you deeply and want you back." The Wells and Chapman families then issued a joint statement thanking him for his support.

On 8th August 2002, the detective leading the hunt urged anyone holding the girls to give them up. In a direct plea, Detective Superintendent David Beck said: "Get in touch with somebody so we can all get the girls home safely." By this time police strongly suspected that the girls had been abducted by someone they knew, but Beck was optimistic that the girls were alive and well. He added: "If someone has taken the girls they might not know what to do next. If the children are with you or you know where they are I would encourage you to contact a solicitor or someone you can rely on. You may have already been thinking of trying to tell someone. Try to see beyond the next few hours, keep in mind your future, the next few days and weeks. Get in touch." At the same time police criticized the £1 million reward for information leading to the girls' safe return. They said the sum, put up by *Express* newspapers, could lead to a wild goose chase and encourage crank callers. A second senior officer added: "A million pounds is a vast sum of money. Unscrupulous individuals could be tempted to invent a sighting to collect part of the reward." *Sunday Express* editor Martin Townsend said: "Our only thought is for the girls' safety."

Police were convinced it would have been too difficult for a stranger to snatch two 10-year-olds from the street without being noticed. All were convinced that Holly and Jessica would have screamed loudly. The police released CCTV footage of the girls' last known movements, while senior officers said all evidence suggested that they went willingly with their captor on the night they disappeared. One detective said: "I can't believe a man, no matter how fit and burly he was, could bundle two girls into a car on his own and get away with it. They would have screamed and struggled. But no one heard anything like that, so we can only conclude that the girls got in the car or van willingly. We don't know if the abductor is someone they have known a long time or if they only met him recently."

Police interviewed schoolfriends to find out who the girls knew and if they had met anyone. They also looked at friends and acquaintances of both sets of parents, and traced and visited scores of paedophiles and people on the sex offenders' register. Meanwhile, CCTV showed the girls walking across the deserted car park of the Ross Peers sports centre near their homes in Soham. They were seen for 46 seconds walking towards the entrance of the centre, next to the town's college and their school. The CCTV clock showed 18.13 when they appeared, but it was believed to be four minutes slow. It appeared that the last time the girls were definitely seen was at 6.45pm, walking towards Soham's war memorial, but an unconfirmed sighting put them at the Q8 garage at the Downfield roundabout in the south of the town, more than a mile from the memorial, at 7.00pm. School caretaker Ian Huntley (28), who lived near the sports centre with his girlfriend Maxine Carr (25), reported that he had seen the girls at about 6.15pm and said they seemed happy, "without a care in the world". He said: "I was outside washing the dog when they stopped. My girlfriend used to teach them last term and they asked me: 'How's Miss Carr?' I told them she wasn't very good because she didn't get the full-time job she applied for. I just saw them for a few moments. They went off towards the library."

On 10th August 2002, police announced that they were following significant new leads based on records from Holly's computer. Expert Gordon Stevenson, the boss of a data recovery firm whose technicians helped convict Gary Glitter and Harold Shipman, explained the tracing process: "When you access the internet on a computer, it keeps track of virtually everything you do. The details would be in temporary files, which are only kept for a few days – but would still be on Holly's computer." Files from further back would have been written over, but the data in them could still be recovered. Skilled technicians would be able to get details of activities within 24 hours, he continued. Given slightly longer, they could also revive apparently deleted material and delve into computerized records from up to two years earlier. Stricter controls on chatrooms were called for by Rachel O'Connell of the Cyberspace Research Unit at the University of Central Lancashire: "Safety features should be included by the chat services provider, like a panic button. The button will connect the computer user to a moderator, employed by the chat service provider. This will alert them that something untoward is going on in the chatroom. Children should also be able to save copies of their conversations and the chat service providers should also save information. This would help to track down who approached the children." At this time, in 2002, around one in five children used a number of the 100,000 chatrooms, and around one tenth of those arranged to meet their cyber friends.

Police still hoped that Holly and Jessica's abductor would make contact. They also confirmed that they did not believe that the girls' disappearance was connected to teenager Milly

Dowler, who had gone missing in March. Milly's parents told the families: "Our hearts go out to you." However, no one surrendered to police and no phone calls had been received. Police admitted they had no suspect and were still waiting for a key piece of evidence to emerge. They also confirmed that they were considering the possibility that two kidnappers were involved. They ruled out an accident because of a lack of evidence to support the theory, and urged the public to keep an eye out for the girls and to remain vigilant. Searches of the waterways around the fens continued, and Detective Superintendent Hankins spoke of the "sheer hell" that the girls' families were going through. "You can all imagine the anguish they are suffering. Our thoughts are with them and we hope and pray for the safe return of Jessica and Holly."

On 12th August 2002 it was revealed that 700 sex offenders in three counties were to be questioned by police. By this time, more than 7,500 people had contacted police during the eight-day search for the children, and police asked neighbouring forces in Suffolk and Norfolk to identify likely suspects. It was thought that Jessica and Holly were still alive. Detective Chief Inspector Andy Hebb told the press: "We are looking at high-risk offenders. They are categorized by the 'risk matrix' system which looks at their age, their previous offences and the type of offences." A search for Jessica's mobile phone also continued, concentrated at the centre of the signal's radius, near a roundabout on the road to Newmarket.

Police received more than 500 calls after a reconstruction of the girls' last known movements was staged, but nothing fruitful emerged until police said that a driver seen struggling with two children in a green car was being sought for questioning. The driver had been spotted by a taxi driver near where the girls went missing, and his car was seen swerving across the road as he thrashed his arms around, even facing backwards while at the wheel. Hebb said: "As a matter of urgency we need to trace this car and its driver. His behaviour is described as bizarre. I think it's an important, significant line of inquiry. I hope it's a breakthrough." On television, Superintendent David Beck said to the kidnapper: "Look deep into the core of your soul and you'll know that what you've done is wrong. Leave the girls somewhere – somewhere safe where they can be found." He continued: "Now is the time to stand tall and look at yourself in the mirror. Things are out of control and I don't think you've planned for it to get this way. You will be justifying to yourself all the reasons and the excuses for what you've done … you will be feeling guilty and fearful for what the future may hold. This is serious. I can't pretend it isn't. But don't let it get worse. There is a way out – there is a way you can still emerge from this with credit. I am asking you to work with me to make that happen … Examine your conscience and you will know that it is right to do that. Stop this now." Meanwhile police launched a nationwide hunt for the driver of the metallic green saloon.

By this time there were 16 police forces working on the

case and while it was not thought that the disappearance of Milly Dowler was connected, the unsolved abduction of a six-year-old girl in Staffordshire in March 2001 was linked to the case. The young child, snatched while playing near her home in Barton-under-Needwood, was sexually assaulted but found half an hour later.

Holly and Jessica's teacher, Joy Pederson (38), was away on holiday when the girls went missing. When she returned she was devastated to hear that two of her pupils had vanished. Fighting back tears, she clutched a thank you card written by one of the victims when she was interviewed by the press. Mrs Pederson had been a teacher at St Andrew's Church of England Primary School for 12 years. She had also taught Holly's brother, Oliver (12), and Jessica's sisters, Rebecca (16) and Alison (14). She confirmed that both girls had been taught internet safety and not to use phone numbers or addresses.

On 13th August 2002, two mounds of freshly dug earth 30 yards apart in woodland close to Newmarket racecourse were investigated by police. Hundreds of detectives and forensic officers were called to the site after a jogger reported "disturbed earth". The two distraught families steeled themselves for the worst. In the nine days since the girls had gone missing they had clung to the hope that their daughters would be found safe and well. This hope wasn't extinguished as police began a huge investigation at the site, but Kim Perks, a Cambridgeshire police spokeswoman, said: "The families have been told to brace themselves for potential bad news. It's a very difficult time for them right now." She added: "The families are in a hell of a state at the thought this could be it." The site was on the edge of a copse in an area known as The Gallops at Warren Hill – less than 10 miles from the girls' homes – set back about 200 yards from the roadside. The investigation was set to be a long process. Detective Chief Inspector Andy Hebb said: "An initial assessment of the site has led us to believe the earth has been recently disturbed. We are mindful of the need to make a full examination." Plastic tents were put up over the two areas and floodlights brought in. Hebb continued: "Forensic scientists have begun their work and if they think it is appropriate they will begin excavating the two sites." Careful work needed to be carried out first and a large number of photographs of the area and the site were taken before any further extensive searches. Despite a prolonged wait for the families, it was essential that the police preserved the potential crime scene.

The driver of the green car had still not come forward, and the police were unable to trace him. Police actions came under scrutiny when it emerged that it had been several days before the taxi driver's account was followed up. Information given to police in a major inquiry has to go through a long process before it ends up in the hands of officers, in which the Holmes computer system is used to spot patterns and highlight tips. In this particular probe, calls to the hotline went through to the normal switchboard at the Cambridgeshire police HQ in

Huntingdon. Calls were then transferred and assessed as high, medium or low priority and sent to an IT room. High-priority calls were taken by hand to the Holmes room, specially set up in a portable building. Calls were logged on to the system and an "action allocation" told the inquiry team which possible leads they needed to follow up. A Holmes statement reader looked at all the entries, searching for links in the information from different callers. Police stressed that if an obviously vital piece of evidence came in, the operator would run to the inquiry room and flag it up personally.

Detective Superintendent David Beck, who sent the abductor voice and text messages via Jessica's mobile phone, urged the man to come forward on 14th August. The mounds of earth near Newmarket proved to be badger setts, not graves, and the senior officer believed the two girls were still alive. By this time a "sighting" of the two girls in the green car had also been ruled out. These developments increased the agony of the two families, who were left clinging to a "glimmer of hope". Beck's personal messages to the kidnapper were thought to be the first of their kind, the main reason for them being "the real desire to bring these children back alive. We mustn't lose that hope."

Over the following two days, the anguish of the girls' families was outlined in the press, particularly the horrifying night they spent waiting to find out if the mounds of earth contained the bodies of their daughters. Despite relief that the girls hadn't been found in the copse, they then had to continue their wait. It was a mix of emotions, and a friend told reporters: "The last 10 days have been almost unbearable." Meanwhile, police insisted that they were following a "number of positive lines of inquiry". However, the kidnapper failed to respond to the police request to contact them before a deadline given by Detective Superintendent Beck.

It was Britain's biggest manhunt, and 426 staff from 21 forces worked flat out. Many officers were working 20-hour days and many more had cancelled leave. By 16th August Acting Deputy Chief Constable Keith Hoddy had formally taken control of the investigation. Cambridgeshire Chief Constable Tom Lloyd called in a senior officer and his team from Scotland Yard's Serious Crime Group to review the inquiry. Kim Perks said: "Now is not the time to be too proud to ask for expert help and advice. They will look at what we have done and if we have missed anything obvious, they will tell us. And they will make sure we have focused on the right areas and the right procedures are in place so we are not delaying things." In Soham, house-to-house inquiries were stepped up; police were convinced that the town must "hold the key".

Cambridgeshire police struggled to cope with the sheer weight of information from the public: around 1,000 phone calls had been coming in each day. Finally, a breakthrough came later on 16th August, when it was revealed that police were questioning a school caretaker and his girlfriend. Nine officers searched the home of Ian Huntley and Maxine Carr in Soham. Search teams also moved into Soham Village College and its grounds, where Huntley worked. The couple were led away by officers at 3.40pm and were quizzed at separate police stations after agreeing to give witness statements. An inquiry source described it as a "highly significant" development in the hunt for the two girls, as Huntley was the last known person to speak to them. He and Carr gave permission for police to hunt their two-storey detached house in the grounds of the college. As uniformed officers arrived to carry out the search, senior detectives said the families had been told of developments. The hunt, which extended to the primary school, was expected to take days rather than hours. Senior officers confirmed that police were convinced the "piece of the jigsaw" they were looking for was close to Soham.

Huntley had started work at the college in December 2001 or January 2002. He had originally been known as Ian Nixon, but had changed his name a few months previously for "family reasons". Police were believed to have become increasingly concerned over his behaviour. He gave a series of emotional interviews about the girls and on *GMTV* on the morning of 16th August, when he said he felt "gutted" that they were still missing: "It doesn't help the fact that I was one of the last people to speak to them, if not the last person to speak to them." He continued: "I keep reliving that conversation and thinking perhaps something different could've been said, perhaps kept them here a little longer and maybe changed events." Talking of the people of Soham, Huntley said: "Overall I think they are coping quite well. The overall view seems to be that while there's no news there's still a glimmer of hope and I'd go along with that." Asked if he personally still had hope for the girls he replied: "Yes, yes." Huntley had helped in the search for the girls the night they went missing.

Maxine Carr was also in the spotlight. The teaching assistant invited the *Mirror* into her home, and said she was distraught at the disappearance of Holly and Jessica. In an interview that was given as pleas were made to possible abductors to let the girls go, Carr recalled Huntley's brief chat with the two girls. The woman who had taught Holly and Jessica for six months at their primary school said: "It's terrible. I only wish we had asked them where they were going. My partner Ian talked to them for a couple of minutes as they came walking past the front of the house. If only we knew then what we know now, then we could have stopped them or done something about it. I was in the bath and he was out washing our German shepherd Sadie in the garden." She continued: "Jessica is more of a tomboy. She loves playing football and swimming. They are both very nice, quiet girls … Holly is more feminine, a bright girl, very good at English."

In another interview with reporters Huntley said: "It seems they have just disappeared off the face of the earth. How can two girls go missing in broad daylight … no sightings, no nothing. It beggars belief."

Police arrested the couple in the early hours of 17th August 2002 on suspicion of murder. It was the first time senior officers feared that the two young girls were dead. The two girls were found later that same day, in a copse at Wangford, near Lakenheath, Suffolk, just a few hundred yards from where Huntley and Carr had previously lived. Holly and Jessica's bodies were taken to hospital from the copse, bringing the horrific search for them to an end. On 19th August, Huntley and Carr were still in custody, after police were given permission by a magistrate to continue questioning them. Carr's mother said: "I can vouch for my daughter and she is innocent."

As the investigation continued, more began to emerge about Huntley. His father Kevin had previously lived in the same cottage as Huntley in the hamlet of Wangford, while his grandmother lived a few miles from the scene. His younger brother, by then married to Huntley's ex-wife, also lived in the area, which comprised a few houses, a Tabernacle Church and a hall. Huntley knew the area, having lived there for a short while. The *Mirror* spoke to Huntley's ex-wife, Claire Evans, who failed to mention when interviewed that she had been married to the suspected murderer before marrying his brother. After telling the newspaper that she said: "It's terrible news. I know the police have to do their job but it's another life wrecked." After giving the interview, she was believed to have left the area for a few days to escape attention.

After leaving school, Huntley drifted between jobs across

Lincolnshire. He struggled to hold on to anything, but one that he did stick with was at a nappy factory in Barton-upon-Humber. Another employer confirmed that he had been known as Ian Nixon.

As the police net closed in on Huntley, the parents of the two murdered children spoke of their grief at losing their "gorgeous" daughters. Sharon and Leslie Chapman said: "We would like to thank everyone for their kindness and support during this very tense and traumatic time, especially friends, family and family liaison officers. While we appreciate your support and all your assistance in this very trying time we would like you to respect our privacy and allow us some time alone."

Nicola and Kevin Wells said: "Although still numb after losing our gorgeous daughter Holly, please accept our heartfelt thanks for everyone's help and support throughout this traumatic fortnight." The news came nearly 30 hours after the bodies were found beside a track on the edge of Lakenheath US airbase in Suffolk. Police believed the bodies had been left there the night the girls went missing. The area was isolated and inaccessible and normally only four-wheel drives would attempt to use it. Teams of forensic experts worked under a protective tent throughout the night and day to secure any evidence they could. Home Office pathologist Dr Nat Cary made a preliminary investigation before the bodies were taken to Addenbrooke's Hospital in Cambridge for further forensic examination. A private ambulance in a convoy of three vehicles emerged through the dense mist, with a marked police car flashing its headlights as it led the way. Samples of DNA were taken from the bodies, while in Soham the car wash at the Q8 garage was sealed off and a bag was removed from a car vacuuming machine.

At a moving press conference, Acting Deputy Chief Constable Keith Hoddy said: "It is with great sadness that I have to tell you the following news. It may be some days yet before we are able to positively identify the two bodies. However, we are as certain as we possibly can be that they are those of Holly and Jessica. Holly and Jessica's families have been told this terrible news. Before I say anything else can I suggest we pause for a moment in silence in memory of these two little girls and out of respect for their families and their many hundreds of friends.

"Holly and Jessica were reported missing on the evening of August 4 and since that time a huge effort has been mounted to find them. We, like the families, refused to give up hope that the girls would be found alive and well. Our heartfelt sympathies go out to Holly's parents and brother and Jessica's parents and sisters at this ghastly time. An enormous effort involving hundreds of police officers supported by civilians and scores of experts worked tirelessly to trace the girls and the sense of sorrow now is felt acutely. Holly's and Jessica's families continue to be supported by trained family liaison officers at this, the bleakest of moments.

"They are being given every possible support and this support will continue in the days, weeks and months to come.

Now is a time for quiet contemplation. It is a time to respect the grief of Holly's and Jessica's families and I ask that you respect their need for privacy."

Outside St Andrew's church, where a moving service dedicated to the girls had been held earlier, there was a sea of flowers. At Lakenheath, another carpet of flowers was left by the public on a mound of grass near the track leading to where the bodies were found. One note said: "To the two Soham angels. May your wings take you to a better world." As the press gathered to survey the scene, one man driving past shouted out of the window: "Hang him!"

On the following Sunday morning, the Reverend Tim Alban Jones greeted more than 500 to St Andrew's church for the 9.30am Holy Communion: he usually expected around 50 parishioners. The sudden storm that erupted as the service began echoed the grim mood of the congregation. A single bell rang out as the people of Soham mourned Holly and Jessica with quiet dignity. In a joint Church of England and Methodist service, Methodist minister Alan Ashton fought back tears as he said: "Lord grant peace to Holly and Jessica, comfort their parents and give strength to us all." The reading from Matthew 15, verses 10–20 included the words: "For out of the heart came evil intentions, murder, adultery, fornication, theft, false witness, slander. These are what defile a person."

Tim Alban Jones spoke of the "searing, heart-rending agony" that the girls' parents were going through, and said:

"Sadly in Soham, we know all too well an appalling example of the depravity to which humans can sink." However, he also described the enormous dignity and courage shown by the families of the two girls. Laid next to the mountain of flowers that were growing by the day in the churchyard was a single pink rose on the rain-soaked grass; the card simply said: "Why?" This was a question that many were asking.

In an exclusive report from journalist Lorraine Fisher, she described how police arrested Ian Huntley at his parents' home in Littleport. She received a call at 3.30am one Saturday morning. "Ian Huntley is at his parents' home and he wants to talk to you. Now." She described how her heart leapt into her mouth: "The chief suspect in Britain's biggest ever manhunt wanted me to interview him. I knew, despite the early hour, I had to go.

"I rushed to the car and set off along the remote, dark roads to his parents' home in Littleport, Cambs. I knew exactly where it was. I had spent the evening with Kevin and Lynda Huntley as they tried to comprehend their eldest son being implicated in such a dreadful crime. They had only just been told their son was being interviewed by police when they arrived back home to find me and another woman reporter waiting to speak to them. Lynda was beside herself with horror, Kevin was calmer and more together. We chatted about Ian – his personality, his background and how he reacted to the girls going missing, among other things. He was a nice lad, they reassured me, and had been very upset when Jessica and Holly disappeared. Around 10pm I gave them the news that Ian had been released without charge. And later, when they told me he had just rung them, I asked if I could interview him.

"At first he refused. But later he called them back to say he wanted to meet me and the other reporter. That promise came to nothing, and, in the early hours, we gave up and went home. I'd only been asleep for half an hour when the call came to say the meeting was back on. But as I drove to Littleport for the interview, a nagging doubt surfaced in my mind. I was about to have a moonlight rendezvous with a possible killer, his father and his brother in their house. I had earlier phoned my boss and been told that under no circumstance should I go into the house without someone waiting outside. My colleague and I decided to call a photographer and ask him along to put our minds at rest.

"When we arrived, Kevin and his other son Wayne, 27, were waiting at the gate for us. 'Come in,' they urged us. 'Ian is waiting for you.'"

The two reporters waited in the car for their photographer colleague to join them. As they reassured Wayne that they wouldn't have to wait much longer, a silver car screeched to a halt in front of them and two men leapt out and asked Wayne who he was. Fisher suddenly realized that they were surrounded by unmarked police cars: the two journalists were in the middle of a dawn raid. They were ordered by an officer to drive to the end of the road and wait there. At that point police stormed the house and arrested the man they suspected of murder. It later transpired that the house had been under surveillance by police before the journalists arrived, and they would never have allowed them to enter the property.

The post mortems failed to discover how Holly and Jessica were killed. The five-hour examinations by Dr Nat Cary were "inconclusive" and further tests were needed, which were likely to take weeks. This blow came as police were expected to ask magistrates for permission to carry on questioning Huntley and Carr. Meanwhile, the gamekeeper who found the bodies of the 10-year-olds looked shaken as he returned to the scene. Keith Pryer (48) had to go back to feed around 300 pheasant fledglings in a pen at the bottom of the dirt track. He had been "very shaken up" by the grim discovery he had made, and clearly still was as he stopped briefly at the wheel of his car to speak to a police officer before entering the crime scene. A local farmer, Brian Rutterford, described how the shocking find had affected Mr Pryer. He said: "He's in a terrible state. What he saw was horrific. He's completely shocked and traumatized." Mr Pryer had barely been able to sleep since he found the girls. "He told me exactly how and where he had found the bodies. It was horrible, not the sort of thing anyone would ever want to see," said Mr Rutterford.

Rosa Prince, one of 10 journalists covering the case for the *Mirror*, wrote on 20th August 2002: "Murder suspect Ian

Huntley bites his fingers anxiously on day four of the hunt for Holly Wells and Jessica Chapman.

"Sitting in a car overlooked by a poster of the girls in their Man United shirts, he looks drawn and anxious. On that day, 8th August, the police released CCTV footage showing the last images of Holly and Jessica wandering around Soham. In interviews with journalists, Huntley told how they walked past his house at Soham Village College at 6.15 as he washed his dog outside. Meanwhile, it also emerged yesterday that Huntley and fiancée Maxine Carr were among the first to see Detective Superintendent David Beck's direct appeal to the kidnappers. The couple helped a journalist who was on a tight deadline and needed to watch a videotape of the appeal, which had just been released by the police but had not yet been broadcast on national television. After letting her in, Huntley put the tape on and the couple watched as Beck said: 'I appeal to you again to work with me to stop this getting any worse than it is. You do have a way out.' Insisting the journalist watch it a second time, Huntley then said: 'It beggars belief.' As the journalists, Harriet Arkell of the *London Evening Standard*, thanked the couple, Huntley added: 'It's no trouble. Anything to help get those two little girls back.' Arkell later said: 'If they were the couple Mr Beck's video appeal was directed at, you would never have guessed. Not a flicker of emotion passed across either of their grey, pallid faces. They just looked, like most people in Soham – exhausted and concerned.'"

On 20th August 2002, caretaker Ian Huntley was charged with the murders of Holly Wells and Jessica Chapman.

Hours earlier he was sectioned under the Mental Health Act 1983 and taken to Rampton high security hospital. On the same day, Carr was charged with attempting to pervert the course of justice. Huntley's case was listed to be heard by Peterborough magistrates on 21st August. A spokesman for Rampton confirmed that they had admitted a 28-year-old for assessment after concerns were expressed with regard to his fitness to be interviewed by police. He was to remain for an undetermined time, and it was up to doctors to decide whether he was capable of standing trial or entering a plea. Psychiatrists had up to 28 days to assess him but could apply for further extensions up to six months or more. It was, however, still possible that a patient deemed to need mental health care could stand trial for murder. Depending on the outcome of assessments, Huntley could have been held at the hospital for up to five years. Having been sent to Rampton, Huntley joined the likes of killers including Beverly Allitt, as well as many of the country's most dangerous criminals. The Mental Health Act 1983 helped doctors deal with patients who were mentally disordered, and on occasion allowed for their compulsory detention and treatment. Huntley was sectioned because he was judged to be suffering from a "mental disorder", a classification that included severe mental impairment, psychopathic disorder or mental illness. A court was satisfied that he posed a potential threat to other

Family doctor Harold Shipman is known to have murdered 218 of his patients, but many believe the number over his career might have been 355.

Sisters (left to right) Betty Clayton, Helen Blackwell, Jayne Gaskell and Brenda Hurst, whose parents Bertha Moss and Sydney Walton were both killed by Harold Shipman.

Harold Shipman had been a practising GP since 1974, and opened his own surgery in Hyde in 1993.

How one newspaper broke the news of Harold Shipman's guilty verdict, with the GP being dubbed Dr Death on 1st February 2000.

Mark Bridger at Mold Crown Court in May 2013 after being found guilty of the abduction and murder of April Jones. The five-year-old had been sighted willingly getting into a vehicle near her home on 1st October 2012.

The memorial card at the funeral of murdered school girl April Jones in Machynlleth, North Wales, 26th September 2013.

April

4th
April
2007

1st
October
2012

St. Peter's Church, Machynlleth
Thursday 26th of September 2013

The *Mirror* asks why it took the police so long to discover that the body of missing teenager Tia Sharp was hidden in her grandmother's house.

Stuart Hazell, Tia's grandmother's partner, pleaded guilty to her murder and was sentenced to life imprisonment on 14th May 2013, with a tariff of 38 years.

The funeral of murdered school girl Tia Sharp reaches the North East Surrey Crematorium in Morden, September 2012.

The area around Fringe Benefits, 47 Southgate Street, Gloucester is cordoned off following the murder of Hollie Gazzard in February 2014. The 22-year-old's ex-boyfriend Asher Thomas Maslin was later charged with her murder.

Floral tributes near the home of Mikaeel Kular in Edinburgh on Ferry Gait Crescent in early 2014. The three-year-old boy went missing from his home in Drylaw on 15th January and his body was later found in woodland in Fife. His mother was charged with his murder.

Daily Mirror

THE MORNING JOURNAL WITH THE SECOND LARGEST NET SALE.

See To-day's 'DAILY MAIL.'

No. 1,286. Registered at the G. P. O. as a Newspaper. FRIDAY, DECEMBER 13, 1907. One Halfpenny.

CAMDEN TOWN MURDER MYSTERY: ROBERT WOOD ON TRIAL FOR HIS LIFE AT THE NEW BAILEY.

The curtain rose on the third act in the Camden Town murder drama yesterday when Robert Wood, an artist, was put in the dock at the Central Criminal Court and tried for the murder of Emily Dimmock on the night of September 11. (1) Robert Wood, the accused man. (2) Emily Dimmock, the murdered woman. (3) Ruby Young, the accused man's sweetheart, who is the principal witness for the prosecution. (4) Mr. Marshall Hall, the leading counsel for the defence. (5) Mr. Arthur Newton, the prisoner's solicitor, who prepared the defence, and who defended Wood during the magisterial hearing. (6) The crowd outside the New Bailey watching the entrance of Ruby Young, who is under one of the umbrellas seen in the photograph. (7) Mr. Justice Grantham, the presiding Judge. (8) Sir Charles Mathews, who is prosecuting on behalf of the Crown.—(Elliott and Fry, Cresswell, Bassano, and London Stereoscopic.)

The principal players in the court proceedings following the murder of Emily Dimmock in September 1907.

Emily Dimmock – also known as Phyllis – was found with her throat cut in St Paul's Road, near King's Cross in North London, on the morning of 12th September 1907.

Marion Gilchrist, brutally murdered during a robbery in Glasgow. Oscar Slater was convicted of the crime but later released and acquitted, after his cause was championed by renowned author Sir Arthur Conan Doyle.

Oscar Slater pictured during his trial at the High Court in Edinburgh.

Two of Bible John's victims: Helen Puttock and
Jemima McDonald.

Peter Tobin, believed
by many to be the
perpetrator behind the
Bible John killings in
the late 1960s, is led
away in May 2007 after
being found guilty of
killing Angelika Kluk
the previous year.

A map showing where two of Robert Black's victims – Caroline Hogg and Susan Maxwell – were snatched.

PORTOBELLO

COLDSTREAM

CAROLINE HOGG disappeared JULY 8

SUSAN MAXWELL disappeared JULY 30, 1982

FOUND: AUGUST 13, '82

UTTOXETER

CHILD'S BODY FOUND JULY 18

TWYCROSS

DAGENHAM

London

The *Mirror* runs a front page on Britain's worst child serial killer in May 1994.

DAILY Mirror HONESTY, QUALITY, EXCELLENCE 20p

CONFESSION OF WORST CHILD SERIAL KILLER

EXCLUSIVE

I did not recognise Di as we dragged man from park lake SEE PAGE 13

LAST RITES FOR JACKIE

MY 40 VICTIMS

SHOCK REPORT SEE PAGES 2, 3, 4, 5, 6, 7, 8 and 9

GENETTE COPS TO QUIZ TRIPLE CHILD KILLER

VICTIM

SO EVIL

Dad hopes for answers on mystery

EXCLUSIVE

Robert Black has been convicted of four murders, but officials believe he is responsible for many more.

Police officers wanted to quiz Black in April 2005 about the disappearance of Genette Tate in August 1978. The 13-year-old's body has never been found.

Forensic investigators
at the scene of James
Bulger's murder in
February 1993.

James Bulger's
father heads the
pall bearers at the
toddler's funeral.

The paper reveals
the faces of evil in
November 1993. Jon
Venables and Robert
Thompson were found
guilty of the murder of
James Bulger, but were
given new identities
on their release from
prison in 2001.

The front of the *Mirror* appeals to missing schoolgirls Holly Wells and Jessica Chapman to phone home in August 2002.

DAILY
Mirror
Tuesday
August 6 2002
NEWSPAPER OF THE YEAR
20p

LOST: A huge search was on last night for Man Utd fans Holly Wells and Jessica Chapman, both 10, of Soham, Cambs

PHONE HOME GIRLS
Police plea to missing 10-year-old Becks fans
FULL STORY: PAGES 4 & 5

Police search the area around Soham for clues to the whereabouts of the missing schoolgirls.

The parents of murdered Soham schoolgirls Holly Wells and Jessica Chapman, (left to right) Nicola and Kevin Wells and Sharon and Leslie Chapman, outside the Old Bailey in London in April 2003.

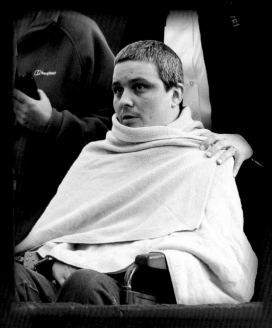

Ian Huntley – convicted of murdering Holly Wells and Jessica Chapman – looking drugged, is taken back to Wakefield prison after a failed suicide bid.

Mick Philpott pictured in happier times with his wife Mairead, mistress Lisa Willis and eight of their children at his home in Derby.

Mick Philpott and his wife Mairead break down in tears at a press conference in Derby in May 2012, following the fire at their home which claimed the lives of six of their children.

Protesters display a banner outside Nottingham Crown Court before the appearance of Mick and Mairead Philpott.

The house at 18 Victory Road in Allenton, Derby, where the six children died in a fire set by Mick and Mairead Philpott, was being prepared for demolition in September 2013.

The front page of the *Mirror* reveals the horrific murder of WPCs Fiona Bone and Nicola Hughes in September 2012.

Police forensic officers at the scene of the shooting in Hattersley, Manchester.

Floral tributes grew quickly at the scene of the double murder of the two women police officers in Mottram Langdale, Hattersley.

Colleagues and members of the public line the streets of Manchester for the funeral of WPC Fiona Bone.

Families of Fiona Bone and Nicola Hughes at Preston Crown Court for the start of Dale Cregan's trial in February 2013. He was charged with the murder of the two police officers.

Armed police officers stand guard outside Preston Crown Court.

The Savage, Dale Cregan, was jailed for life in June 2013 for the murder of Fiona Bone and Nicola Hughes.

people, or to himself. At first Huntley was held under Section 4 (meaning he could be detained for 72 hours), before this was adjusted to Section 2 (where he could be held for 28 days).

The atmosphere in Court One at Peterborough Magistrates' Court was tense. A haggard and ghostly pale Maxine Carr appeared nervous and bewildered. The charge against her was read out: "between August 9, 2002 and August 18 in the County of Cambridgeshire with intent to pervert the course of public justice you did a series of acts which had the tendency to pervert the course of public justice, in that you gave false information to police officers in a criminal investigation and that is contrary to common law". Carr listened intently, but was overwhelmed when it was revealed that the charge carried a maximum sentence of life imprisonment. At this point psychiatrists ruled that Huntley was not fit to appear in court. Carr was informed by the chair of the bench, Gill Wild, that she would be sent to Peterborough Crown Court for trial. An angry crowd of at least 500 people which had assembled outside exploded in fury as the accused woman was driven away from the hearing. Some people banged on the side of the police van in which she was transported, while some jeered, and others stood silently, holding up pictures of Holly and Jessica. The crowd applauded Detective Chief Inspector Andy Hebb as he left the court. Later it was revealed that Carr was being kept under a suicide vigil at Holloway prison in north London where she was being held, while Huntley was under a round-the-clock watch.

Holly and Jessica's parents all asked to visit the site where their daughters' bodies were found. This visit took place the day after the bodies had been formally identified.

By 24th August the possibility that Carr could face further charges had not been ruled out by the coroner, but while the "severely decomposed and partially skeletalized" bodies of Holly and Jessica did not reveal the secret of how they died, it was confirmed that they didn't die where they were discovered. An interim report by Dr Nat Cary stated that the bodies were so badly damaged they could only be identified by DNA testing. Coroner David Morris confirmed that he had granted a request from Jessica's parents that their daughter's body should be cremated and from Holly's parents that she should be buried. Both funerals were to remain private. Two days later, the football shirts worn by the murdered girls were being tested for crucial DNA evidence. Their trainers were also tested by forensic experts after the items of clothing were found by police. On 29th August, at a preliminary hearing, Carr gave evidence by videolink from prison to avoid angry mobs outside Peterborough Crown Court. The extremely sensitive case had garnered so much media interest that even Carr's mother and Huntley's family had to stay away from work and home respectively. What worried Carr's lawyer was that the media had not made it clear that she was not accused of the murders or of abduction. Public fury at her part in the case was evident, and Carr received death threats from other inmates in Holloway.

The following day a service at Ely Cathedral was one of celebration and remembrance for Holly and Jessica. The service was put together by the two families. The Reverend Tim Alban Jones, in tribute to the two girls, said: "We have seen strangers and friends weeping together in shared grief and anguish. We have seen the dedication and diligence of hundreds of police officers. We have seen our town of Soham united in common grief, and we have seen the extraordinary bravery, courage and dignity of two sets of parents. All of this is a direct result of the way that Holly and Jessica have touched the hearts and lives of so many people. It is surely fitting that we are gathered here to pay tribute to them … Holly and Jessica were both living children. They had been friends since they were very small children and had grown up together as members of two loving families. They were brought up to know and treasure the value of love."

Huntley was said to be allowed only one newspaper a day in order to follow Carr's case and what the press had to say about him. He was described as quiet and moody, and was said to have refused to speak for a week after he was arrested. By the end of August he was on hunger strike. Staff at the secure hospital said he had "sunk into a deep depression".

On 2nd September 2002, Jessica Chapman was laid to rest. Holly Wells' funeral followed the next day. England captain David Beckham sent flowers to both private funerals.

On 6th September, Huntley's house stood screened from

view from children attending Holly and Jessica's school by a roof-high green fence – eventually the fence was surrounded by trees as police continued their search inside. It was decided that the sight of it would be too painful for all the youngsters, especially Holly's brother Oliver and Jessica's sister Alison, as they returned to school after the summer break. Four days later Huntley was due in court for the first time, and people were urged by police to stay away. The short hearing was designed to bring him "under the jurisdiction of the courts" for the first time. However, the angry mob was back as a silent Huntley stood in the dock.

Huntley stood charged with the murders of Holly and Jessica, and a new count of conspiring to pervert justice with Carr. In Rampton, he was said to be living a "comfortable" life. By 9th October, however, he had been moved from the high security hospital to Woodhill prison, after psychiatrists ruled he was not suffering from a mental illness and was fit to stand trial. He was seen a day earlier in his third court appearance at Peterborough Crown Court. Woodhill was where Huntley was put under "intensive assessment, observation and study", alongside some of the most complex personalities in the prison system. One of his fellow inmates included kidnapper and killer Michael Sams.

Huntley and Carr were again quizzed by police on 18th October 2002. They were then returned to their respective prisons. Just under a month later, it was revealed that they would go on trial at the Old Bailey, as a judge had ruled that Britain's top court would be preferable to one in East Anglia, amid fears that jurors could have links to the investigation.

The couple had sent each other scores of love letters, but in mid-December 2002, Carr wrote to Huntley ending the relationship.

In January 2003, Carr faced two new charges of lying to police. On 16th April, the parents of both girls faced Huntley and Carr in court when the accused appeared in the dock together for the first time. The two devastated families were accompanied by family liaison officers to Court One. In court, Huntley admitted he had lied to police about the girls, but he denied murdering them. He pleaded guilty to conspiring to pervert the course of justice, but he pleaded not guilty to murder. Carr denied plotting to pervert the course of justice and helping an offender. Both were remanded in custody until the trial in October 2003. It was thought that around 300 people could be called to give evidence.

In early October, Huntley was in an induced coma in hospital after a 29-pill overdose. He was found having a fit in his cell at 3am after taking antidepressants that he had hidden in teabags. His suicide attempt followed an earlier bid three weeks prior. As he lay on life support, it was suspected he might have suffered brain damage; an overdose of the tricyclic that Huntley was taking could have proved fatal. Doctors confirmed that the induced coma meant that Huntley was on life support while his body was completely shut down. He was to be induced out of the coma after about 24 hours.

After surviving his suicide attempt, Huntley was monitored round the clock and was given access to "listeners", specially trained by the Samaritans to talk to him. These listeners were closely monitored during their occasional visits. Two guards were on duty outside his cell at all times, while three CCTV cameras were trained on the interior – theoretically not leaving an inch of it unobserved. He was confined and segregated away from other inmates. One prison source told the *Mirror* that: "Huntley was in an almost unique position in that he had virtually no contact with the rest of the prison. But this created its own problems. He was so isolated there was a danger of him getting depressed and harming himself." Staff were keen to ensure that Huntley would be well enough to stand trial. However, pressure on them to watch Huntley in eight-hour shifts had an impact on other prisoners and staff. Woodhill was already suffering from officer shortages, aggravated, according to a report, by "high sickness levels". The accused man's suicide bid seriously threw the trial into doubt, and gave further anguish to the parents and families of the two murdered girls. A police source said: "We are desperate for this trial to go ahead. The families have been through enough already – this must be torture for them."

Huntley was returned to jail on 10th June 2003. Calls that he should never be allowed to attempt suicide again came from all quarters. Claire, his ex-wife, said: "Now Ian is back in jail is this going to happen again? People, especially the families of Jessica and Holly, need to know the truth. If Ian again tries to kill himself, it will never come out." Home Secretary David Blunkett was said to be "livid" at what was described as a "glaring security lapse" at Woodhill. As Huntley's health improved, the families of the victims issued a statement which read: "We are reassured to hear he is still expected to stand trial at the Old Bailey in October."

It emerged that Huntley had written to a penpal that suicide had crossed his mind. He was said to be feeling particularly lonely and depressed after a request to leave his isolation cell was refused. He wrote: "I have had some feedback regarding my requests to go on a normal location and or some form of association. The answers to both were no, as they say they are fearful for my safety." In July 2003 it was announced that he would be moved to a special cell block before his murder trial, consisting of a six-room suite designed to give foolproof security, at Belmarsh jail in southeast London.

One month before the trial was due to start, Huntley sought to have his trial postponed as barristers argued they had not had enough time to prepare their case. In late September a judge at the Old Bailey agreed a new start date of 3rd November. Just a few days later, it was announced that the judge, jury and both legal teams would visit Soham on 10th November. Huntley and Carr also had a legal right to attend. All three schools in the area – St Andrew's, Weatheralls and the Village College would close that day. On 11th October 2003, Huntley was moved to the ultra-secure cell in Belmarsh and the pre-trial hearing took place 16 days later.

On 3rd November, Kevin and Nicola Wells and Leslie and Sharon Chapman walked sombrely to court at the Old Bailey as jury selection for the three-month trial of Huntley got underway. All four parents braved the barrage of cameras with quiet dignity before taking their seats in Number One court. Huntley and Carr were led in to sit in the dock with a security officer sitting between them. Press and the public were barred from the hearing, but the media were allowed to watch the jury selection process by videolink. The prosecutor, Richard Latham, QC, was expected to make his opening speech the following day. Huntley was to be represented by Stephen Coward, QC, while Carr was represented by Michael Hubbard, QC. The trial judge, Mr Justice Moses, warned potential jurors that they would have to forget all they may have heard or thought about the Soham case and try it on the evidence in court. He said that Huntley and Carr were innocent until proven guilty.

The court heard how Holly and Jessica "fell into the hands" of Huntley within 15 minutes of leaving home. What happened next was known only to the "calculating and manipulative" school caretaker, the Old Bailey heard. The prosecution said Huntley would not deny that the 10-year-old friends died while they were alone with him in his house, and he was also expected to admit he took the girls' bodies to where they were found 13 days later. Richard Latham, QC, told the jury of seven men and five women: "The prosecution case is that these two girls fell into the hands of Huntley shortly after leaving home. For some reason known only to him, he chose to murder them both." Carr then provided him with "support for a wholly dishonest account of his movements and actions," Mr Latham said: "It was a convincing and cold-blooded course … involving repeated lies throughout the period of the girls' disappearance and her arrest." Huntley, he said, was "trying to get away with murder". It transpired that a phone expert had retraced the girls' route, checking for hotspots in Soham, and according to this testing, the signal from Jessica's mobile phone had last come from outside Huntley's house. Huntley maintained he was not guilty of murder, but the QC said: "We will invite you to find that he's guilty. We assert that after the deaths Huntley knew what he was doing. He could remember, understand. He was a man who, insofar as anyone who has killed two 10-year-old girls can be described as rational, was acting rationally. There is evidence of a calculating and manipulative individual who knew precisely what he was up to." Mr Latham continued that the focus of the trial was likely to concentrate on whether or not "it could be construed that the deaths while he was there with them in his house amounted to murder". He told the jury that between 6.30pm and 10.30pm Huntley's movements were unknown. He would only have taken an hour and a half to drive to the spot where the girls were found, and had more than enough time for this in the four hours during which he wasn't seen. Carr's barrister confirmed that it wasn't being suggested that she was directly involved in the murders, but that her alleged role was to "devise a dishonest account of events", to distance Huntley from what he had done. The jury was then told that Huntley had hidden the bodies where he thought they would never be found. Latham told the court that after killing the girls, Huntley had been careful to get them "well away from the scene". Just hours after dumping the bodies, he calmly showed a police officer around the grounds at the school, and even joined in the search for the missing children. Huntley was described as "hovering" while the police conducted their initial search for Holly and Jessica, which became "a feature of his behaviour from now onwards". He was said to have wanted to know what was going on and who knew what, but he didn't want to mix with other local residents who were desperate to help. The first sighting of him after Holly and Jessica disappeared was by a group of three men on a footpath when he denied having seen the youngsters, however. At this point, the prosecution said he was working out a strategy. He hadn't yet had time to talk to Carr.

The fact that Huntley was helping police by opening the college when the search began, talking to them, staying around and generally appearing useful was remarkable, given that he had just killed two children and dumped their bodies. Mr Latham said that when Huntley eventually admitted he had seen Holly and Jessica he was already "developing a defence in his mind". Witnesses also said his red Fiesta was missing from its usual parking place outside his house that night.

Next under the spotlight was Carr, who told "repeated lies" with cold-blooded intent from the time Holly and Jessica disappeared to her arrest almost a fortnight later, the Old Bailey heard. She eventually admitted to police that she had been more than 100 miles away in Grimsby. Mobile phone records of calls between the two accused exposed her lies. She had travelled from Cambridgeshire to Grimsby on 3rd August and planned to stay with her mother for a week. The trip was cut short by the events in Soham, and she returned home on Tuesday 6th August. The telephone evidence was deemed to be significantly important in the prosecution's case. Carr was also spotted with her mother in Grimsby on both the Saturday and Sunday of that weekend. The court heard how Carr had grown close to Holly and Jessica when she was a teaching assistant in their class at St Andrew's primary school – she was even pictured holding a card that Holly had given her when she left the school during the search for the girls. She had failed to gain a full-time post at the school when teaching staff became concerned that she could not "create an appropriate distance" between herself and the children. The prosecution urged the jury to view this as inexperience rather than something more sinister. The court was told how the two girls were "loyal to each other" and would have kicked up a fuss if necessary.

On 6th November 2003, the court heard how the clothes of Holly and Jessica were found partially burned in a rubbish bin at the school where Huntley was caretaker. Among them were the girls' Manchester United tops – which they had been photographed wearing just 90 minutes before they went missing. Head hairs matching Huntley's were mixed up with the clothing and his fingerprints were on a bin liner. All the girls' clothing was found at the bottom of the bin, including their trainers and underwear. Each item had been cut off. The five yellow bins were stored inside during the summer holidays, and it was in the third of them that the evidence came to light. Huntley's fingerprints were found on a new liner, beneath which the clothes were hidden. He made a series of blunders after the disappearance of Holly and Jessica, the jury was told. He "sanitized" his car the day after the murders by cleaning the vehicle inside and out, changing its tyres and replacing the carpet in the boot and the seat covers. Even the receipt for the new tyres had been destroyed in an attempt to disguise what he had done. The car had not long passed an MOT, and the mechanic noted that all the original tyres were well within the legal limit; they were expensive tyres that would have not needed replacing for some time. However, the prosecution argued that tracks in the mud near where the bodies were found would have given Huntley away, providing forensic evidence that he was at the site where the girls' bodies were left. Huntley also cleaned up his house, which according to one police officer smelt strongly of a lemon cleaning fluid in the days after the girls went missing, and hung washing on the line, even though it was raining. He quizzed police closely on several occasions about how long DNA lasts and the size of the search area, and made "slip of the tongue" remarks about the girls' clothing at a press conference and about other details to a hitch-hiker he picked up. In the days after the girls went missing, Huntley was asked by a police officer how he felt. He said: "What can you say? It's dreadful, you know. I just pray as I am sure everybody else does that they are alive and well, you know. Morale has got low around here but everyone is clinging on to a glimmer of hope that everything is fine. I don't think I can speak for the community. The people I have spoken to are very down. Some people are holding out very little hope but there is always hope and that is what everyone has to cling on to." He said abduction "was a possibility", but added: "The environment round here is very dangerous. Anything could have happened. You can't say exactly what you think has happened because you don't know." He claimed the area was plagued with boy racers, "who went joyriding and left chip paper wrappers lying around".

In other interviews Huntley declared the police had "done a magnificent job". An ITN broadcast following a public meeting was played in court, in which the accused was heard telling the interviewer that it had been a good gathering in which a lot of questions had been answered. He also said that they had been advised to think of any strange behaviour they might have seen and to look at their neighbours. He said: "There's only so much you can do without being intrusive." The following day Huntley gave another interview to GMTV, in which he said it was strange there was still so little information about the girls' disappearance. He added: "You would have thought somebody would have seen or heard something. It's very strange." During the search Huntley asked the police about DNA evidence on more than one occasion. He also made up the story that he had seen a man carrying a bin bag the day after the girls disappeared. The prosecution stated that the accused could not be sure whether he had been seen or not, so he invented the sighting in case a witness came forward, to cover himself. A neighbour reported seeing Huntley and Carr looking in the boot of his Fiesta in the days following the disappearance. Carr was crying. When they saw the neighbour, she bowed her head, but continued to sob.

Journalist Brian Reade has written many poignant and thought-provoking articles about some of the worst murders to occur in Britain. He is particularly sensitive to the plight of the parents and families of murdered children. Writing in the Mirror in 2003 he said: "What strikes you most about the parents is their ... composure in the face of such heart-crushing pain. And that leaves those of us on the ... Old Bailey benches beside them feeling so small and weak. Having to sit in a bare, dimly-lit, oak-panelled room full of suits and strangers, seeing the man who admits he was with your dead children in their final hours and a woman accused of being his accomplice, while men in wigs re-live the deaths … must be utterly surreal." He continued: "When the accused are shown on video pleading for whoever had their daughters to return them safely, when Huntley is heard calling them 'just great kids' and Carr calls your girl 'a little angel', the urge to show your despair and rage must be massive. And when you see a graphic of a bin with your little girl's underwear visible, underwear you hear had been 'cut from her body', it must hit like a dagger to your heart." Reade said: "We like to think the worst of their agony is over, because they don't let their eyes get wet, but how do we know they aren't crying inside? We like to think they are strong because it means if it happened to us we too might be that strong. But what we can't imagine is how a part of them is forever dead. It shows in their pale and empty faces … Last August they looked anxious and lost. Today they look focused on what needs to be done."

In court, it transpired that it was Maxine Carr who scrubbed the kitchen at the couple's home. A junior caretaker at Soham Village College who had been helping Huntley unlock buildings on the site went back to 5 College Close for a drink, and saw Carr scrubbing at tiles before preparing to clean the floor. But in a TV interview, she claimed she had no idea what had happened to the girls. She told the interviewer that she had been in the bath – at home – when the girls called round to see her. Mr Latham suggested: "This wasn't someone who on the spur of the moment decided to tell a lie that was instantly regretted. Here we suggest she was entering into the spirit of things and inventing not only an incident but giving it a feeling of truth ..."

The trial also covered the fact that Huntley returned to the bodies three days after he had moved them to the isolated wood, to set fire to the corpses. The prosecution said that the most likely cause of death was suffocation and that sexual assault could not be ruled out. Holly and Jessica were lying side by side wearing their necklaces when they were found in the makeshift grave, the Old Bailey heard. Mr Latham said: "We will have to examine the mind of the man who selected this site and chose to drive the considerable distance in order to use it. If he had been in a blind panic there are plenty of places before you get there to dump bodies." The QC told the court that Huntley had been clever in choosing the spot, as there had been a "very significant possibility" they would never have been found. He said: "There was some preserved skin and hairs on the backs of the bodies. There was no evidence of any compressive neck injury but a positive cause of death in each case was impossible to determine because of the state of the bodies." The pathologist had established, however, that there was no bloodstaining on the clothing, so they excluded stabbing or other significant trauma. There was no evidence of poisoning or the administration of drugs. The prosecution claimed that the burning of the bodies – which only affected the upper half of each – was done to destroy identities or to destroy forensic evidence. Despite the change of tyres, the unusual mixture of concrete and chalk found on the track leading to the bodies was found on the underside of Huntley's Fiesta. An expert scientist who tested pollen grains from the area – some of which were quite rare – found matches with the accused's car and shoes. All experts agreed that the girls were killed on the night they went missing, were dumped soon afterwards and that the accused returned to the site in the following days to set fire to the bodies. On the Wednesday, three days after Holly and Jessica went missing, he was seen with a red petrol can – usually kept in the hangar where the bins were found – in his office. He also had links to the area, and his car showed traces of having been on or near the track. He changed his car tyres, he changed the carpet in the boot and the seat covers. He also lied about Carr being in the house on the fateful night. An extensive search of the house had included the furnishings, floorboards, kitchen units, plasterboard, bathroom fittings, door and window frames. Although no fingerprints were found, fibres were found after detailed examination. Fifteen fibres from Holly and Jessica's clothing were found on Huntley's yellow shirt, which was in the bedroom, and on his beige trousers. There were also fibres found on his fleece, jacket, the left boot which was taken from him in custody, his car boot carpet, the bath mat, the main bedroom carpet, the living room carpet, the hallway carpet, the stairs, the main bedroom cupboard, a seat cover, dusters, the main bedroom duvet and a sheet. The reason that so many were found indicated that the Manchester United shirts shed short fibres when they were cut. In all, 49 fibres were found on 20 different items.

The court also heard how Huntley wrote a crib sheet for Carr so that she could remember what lies to tell. It read: "4.55pm to 5pm, got in bath approx." The jury was told that the card had been altered to read: "5.40 to 5.45 dog home approx. 6.15 girls. 6.25 came down to put tea on." Carr confessed to police that she had repeatedly lied during the 13-day search because she thought Huntley was going to be falsely accused of killing the girls. She said that he had been wrongly accused of an offence before he met her, and he feared that would happen again because he was the last to see the 10-year-olds alive. The prosecution argued that the crib proved the charges of assisting an offender and conspiracy to pervert the course of justice, and stated that Carr either knew or believed that he had committed the killings. She obstructed the police inquiry by maintaining the story for two weeks, distracting the police enough for them to exclude Huntley when they should have been looking at him more carefully. She told lies to the press; she told lies to the police; she told lies to the public. The prosecution argued that it wasn't up to Carr to presume Huntley innocent, and in summing up stated that she did indeed pervert the course of justice. Huntley had told Carr the day after the girls went missing that they had been in the couple's home, and he was the last person to see them alive. However, the jury were told that they should only consider verdicts on Carr if they convicted Huntley of murder.

The court then heard how Huntley invited the girls into the house because one of them had a nosebleed. He told Carr: "One of the girls had gone upstairs holding her nose over the sink in the bathroom." The other child had allegedly gone upstairs and sat on the edge of the bed. In taped telephone conversations with Huntley's mother, Carr admitted as much while on remand in Holloway prison. It showed that she knew on 5th August, well before she began lying, that the girls had been in the house and that both had been upstairs with Huntley.

On 10th November 2003, the jury retraced the steps of the two friends before they died. They followed the route the girls took, visited the hangar where Huntley was accused of trying to destroy the clothing, and on the second day visited the remote spot where the bodies were discovered. As a chill wind blew across the bleak countryside, Richard Latham, QC, dropped his voice and pointed to where strands of Jessica's hair were found hanging from a broken twig. Pointing to the base of the ditch where the girls' bodies were said to have been found side by side, with parts of their arms and legs crossed, he said: "The bodies, therefore, were found just down there. Feel free to have a look ..."

On 1st December 2003, Ian Huntley wept as he took the witness stand and admitted: "I'm responsible for the deaths of Holly and Jessica." There was then a long silence in Number

One court as the man fought to maintain his composure. He sniffed constantly as he finally said: "I wish I could turn back the clock. I wish I could do things differently. I wish none of this had ever happened. I'm sorry for what's happened and I'm ashamed of what I did ... but there's nothing I can do about it now. I sincerely wish there was." When asked if he intended to kill Holly and Jessica he answered no. Earlier, Huntley had told the court that he had been preparing to bath his German shepherd dog – who had run away from him over muddy fields – when the girls arrived. He had invited them inside when Holly had a nosebleed. It got no better so they went to the bathroom. He said: "I went to pass Holly some more tissue and as I did, I'm not really sure how it happened, I sort of turned and then I either slipped or lost my footing or something, and sort of went forward in the direction of Holly." Jessica said: "You pushed her", and he put his hand over her mouth to muffle her screaming. Huntley then let go of Jessica and she fell to the floor, partly in the bathroom and partly in the doorway. He pulled motionless Holly from the bath, became aware of Jessica again and checked them both for signs of life. He agreed he had not tried resuscitation and claimed he hadn't known what to do. He said he had considered calling the police but couldn't believe what had happened. He said: "At the time, things were not clear in my head. I could not think how it happened." Huntley claimed he had acted on "the spur of the moment" and had not meticulously planned how to dispose of the 10-year-olds' bodies. He said that after realizing both girls were dead he sat for several minutes on the landing surveying the scene. Then he picked up Jessica and took her downstairs before going back upstairs for Holly. He said the girls were still wearing their clothing when he moved them. He drove close to where his father used to live in Wangford and drove down Common Drove, where he spied a convenient ditch and decided to dump the bodies there. The bank was too steep to carry the children down, so he rolled them into it. He denied disturbing their clothing in any way before dumping the bodies. He also denied a sexual assault on either of the girls. He said he removed the clothes before he set fire to the bodies.

On 2nd December, Huntley admitted to suffocating Jessica Chapman as he tried to stifle her screams. He agreed that he hadn't given the 10-year-old a chance to survive as she fought for her life, also that she would have desperately struggled for breath after he placed his hand over her mouth, and that her death throes would have lasted longer than 10 seconds. Even so, he denied deliberately killing her, and also denied that Jessica was screaming because he was holding Holly under the bathwater. However, Huntley had to admit that by placing his hand over Jessica's mouth he knew he was starving her of oxygen and, as the counsel put it, she was starting, "in effect, to die". Huntley also had to admit that he was possibly restraining Jessica with his other hand as he suffocated her. Despite Huntley's claims that he couldn't remember what his other hand was doing, the prosecutor made it clear that he must have known that he was killing the child. He was accused of a "ruthless" and calculated cover-up after the deaths. Within minutes, Huntley was hatching a plan to dispose of the bodies, and for the next 13 days he tried to cover his tracks and mislead police. Mr Latham described the dumping of the bodies as "like a military operation" in which Huntley, who had a choice, chose to "cover up". Mr Latham also suggested that it would have taken anywhere up to a minute for Jessica to die of suffocation, and that Huntley deliberately used the hand that was not covering her mouth to stop her head from turning away, so she couldn't free herself. He described how the young child would have fought for her life. Of the deaths, Huntley said: "One was an accident and the other one wasn't deliberate … one died as a result of my inability to act and the other died as a direct result of my actions." The exchanges between prosecutor and the accused became increasingly heated as Mr Latham suggested that the only way Holly could have drowned was if Huntley deliberately held her underwater. He also stated that Jessica was screaming because the man was murdering her friend.

Despite cutting off the girls' underwear – which Huntley claimed he did because of fibre traces – he denied there was any sexual motive for the killings. However, he had tried to point police in the initial stages of their inquiry towards Michael Curtin, who had lost his job as caretaker at the school for inappropriate behaviour with children, and Latham argued that by naming the man, Huntley was implying there was a sexual motive to the killings. The accused agreed, though, that he had been "cold and cynical" by giving media interviews in the days after the girls' disappearance, and raised false hope. Huntley admitted that he had approached Mr Wells to offer support, even though he had not long rolled the desperate father's daughter into a ditch, having killed her.

Meanwhile, Carr described Huntley as an abusive man, controlling and manipulating. In a dramatic outburst, she turned on him: "I am not going to be blamed for what that thing in the box has done to me or those children." In the witness stand, however, she admitted to giving Huntley a false alibi.

The prosecution stuck to their evidence that Holly and Jessica were murdered by Huntley in a ruthless sexually motivated crime. In his closing speech, Mr Latham said that Huntley's behaviour was "cold and calculating", and pointed to the press conference held when the accused told Holly's father, Kevin Wells, "I hope everything turns out OK." The QC said: "To be able to be concerned, that was quite ruthless, that was quite deliberate and it was calculated. This whole business in the house was motivated by something sexual but whatever he initiated with one or the other or both girls plainly went wrong and thereafter, in this ruthless man's mind, both girls simply had to die." The prosecutor also pointed out that the girls would not have gone into the house unless they believed

Carr had been there. They knew her well and felt safe with her. Mr Latham accused Huntley of carrying out "a series of ruthless acts" in dumping the bodies in a remote spot and then cutting their clothes off them, because he was worried about carpet fibres which could link them to his house. He said that Huntley then embarked on "12 days of cynical deception". He helped in the search, spun lies about a suspicious man and, along with Carr, gave media interviews in which they told lies. Mr Latham continued: "He is a capable and convincing liar and you are entitled to bear that in mind. The principle applies to both defendants when you are looking at the media interviews. Note the chatty relaxed manner as she lied through her teeth." Huntley consistently denied being involved in the girls' deaths until presented with crucial forensic evidence – a façade he kept up until eight months after his arrest. He had lost his temper in the witness box under cross-examination and yet maintained control over himself. Mr Coward, QC, barrister for Huntley, said there could be a manslaughter case to answer to, but denied that his client was guilty of murder. He said that Huntley made a string of errors. Carr's QC said his client was a victim of Huntley's "incalculable evil". He told the court that Maxine Carr adored the children in her former care and that they in turn adored her. He said it was preposterous to suggest that she would conceal what Huntley had done if she had worked out he murdered the girls. He said that Carr always maintained that she lied to protect the accused, the man she had loved, from revelations coming out about his past. Mr Justice Moses warned jurors not to let the emotion of the case interfere with their judgment, and told them that it was for them alone to decide the truth. He went on to explain there were three possible verdicts against the accused – guilty of murder, guilty of manslaughter by gross negligence and not guilty. To be guilty of murder he had to have intended to kill the girls or cause serious bodily harm. He also reminded the jury that the pathologist who conducted the girls' post mortems concluded it would be "vanishingly rare" for Huntley's account of the deaths to be true. On 15th December 2003, the jury was sent home after failing to agree verdicts. They had, at this stage, had two days to consider the evidence.

On 18th December, the *Mirror* reported that on the day Huntley killed the two girls, Carr was out looking for sex with other men. The revelations came as Huntley was jailed for life for killing Holly and Jessica. Carr was given three and a half years for conspiring to pervert the course of justice. She was cleared of two charges of assisting an offender. Jailing the pair – convicted on 11–1 verdicts – Mr Justice Moses said that Huntley "showed no mercy and no regret". He slammed the convicted man's "persistent cruelty and merciless cynicism" to the girls' families, adding: "Your tears have never been for them, only for yourself." Meanwhile, Home Secretary David Blunkett ordered an inquiry into how blunders by Humberside police enabled Huntley to get his job as caretaker. Checks when he applied for the job had failed to reveal several rape and indecent assault allegations that Carr had tried to cover-up, three other rape accusations, one of indecently assaulting an 11-year-old girl and three complaints of underage sex in the Immingham and Grimsby area.

Huntley was diagnosed as a psychopath who felt "nothing" by experts at Rampton high security hospital, and psychiatrists believed the double child-killer, who showed no emotion as he was jailed for life, had no mercy and no guilt. A source told the *Mirror*: "He is capable of the most extreme anti-social acts without suffering the consequences. He has no remorse. He is not mad, he knows what he did is wrong. But where others would face crippling emotional consequences, he feels nothing." It had taken the jury 17 hours and 32 minutes to find him guilty of murder. No one knew how Huntley had done it. No one knew why. It was expected that Huntley would remain at Belmarsh until 2004, and then be transferred to Wakefield prison in Yorkshire, rather than being sent to a mental hospital.

Before the murders Huntley had been probed on 10 occasions by police. In 1995 there was an allegation of unlawful sexual intercourse with a 15-year-old girl, and later that year there was an allegation of burglary and theft against him. In March 1996, he admitted his part in breaking into a neighbour's house, but failed to turn up in court. In April 1996, there was another allegation of unlawful sexual intercourse with a 15-year-old girl, and in May 1996 an allegation of unlawful sexual intercourse with a girl of 13. This latter case was dropped. In February 1997, he was arrested for failure to pay fines, and in April 1998 there was an allegation of rape by an 18-year-old. The case was dropped by the CPS. Later that year, an allegation emerged of an indecent assault on a girl of 11, but again the case was dropped. In 1999 it was alleged that he had raped a 17-year-old in Grimsby, but the case was dropped after police decided there was insufficient evidence. In July that same year, there was an allegation of rape by another 17-year-old girl, but Carr provided Huntley with an alibi. However, one woman told the newspapers that she had been brutally raped by Huntley, virtually on her own parents' back doorstep. He had held her down, ripped her tights off and moved her underwear to one side in order to viciously assault her. Another young woman, who had had a relationship with the murderer, told the press how he had once thrown her down a flight of stairs when she told him she thought she might be pregnant. She had left Huntley a few weeks previously after a catalogue of abuse; he had already beaten her unconscious with a pool cue while they lived together in Immingham. The girl was just 16 years old at the time. She described how she had tried to leave him before but that he had tried to kill himself, so she had gone back to him.

Chantel Lea was imprisoned and starved by Huntley when she lived with him as a young teenager. She dated the killer for six months when she was only 15. It ended when he locked her in their dingy bedsit and starved her for two weeks.

She collapsed because of malnourishment, dehydration and exhaustion and was taken to hospital. She did not contact police until she discovered Huntley had been arrested for the murders of Holly and Jessica.

Huntley persuaded a 15-year-old girl to give up school and get a job in a factory while he sat at home. The girl, who gave birth to Huntley's daughter in 1998, was also a victim of his abuse and was beaten for the smallest of misdemeanours: he even slapped her when a pizza was burnt. The pair moved into a bedsit together despite protests from her parents. He then began bullying and controlling the girl, telling her whom she could talk to and what she could and couldn't do. He finally stopped the girl seeing her family, and told her parents that she didn't want to speak to them. He wouldn't let her take their calls. In another story, Huntley erupted in fury when she refused his demands for sex, and grabbed her and pushed her around on several occasions – it convinced her that the killer was a man to be avoided.

The stories were always the same. Women adored Huntley until his violence and control came to the fore. He would then sexually abuse, physically abuse, psychologically abuse and assault the women in his life. Many admitted to having been "swept away" by Huntley at first, but in many cases, he convinced young girls he was younger than he was. Many now describe him as evil. Many had lucky escapes.

By August 2002, the cracks were beginning to show in

Huntley and Carr's violent relationship. When Carr went to Grimsby on 3rd August 2002, it was the first time she had been apart from the killer since she met him in 1999. Both used the time apart to search for new partners. Carr went out partying and Huntley tried to take a neighbour out, but the married mother rejected his advances. Huntley and Carr rowed on the phone just minutes before Huntley murdered Holly and Jessica, and police believe he murdered the two girls in a fit of anger, jealousy and sexual frustration. Huntley had subjected Carr to savage beatings, and according to one ex-colleague enjoyed humiliating her in front of other staff at the school.

In the days following the killer's conviction it emerged that he had been bullied at school, but joined a gang and became a bully himself. He stole from shops and robbed sailors who were too drunk to fight back. He strangled his bull terrier puppy in front of mates because it disobeyed him, and he performed sex acts on a paedophile at £5 a time. He took drugs from the age of 13 and sought out underage girls for sex. According to one former friend, Huntley knew that one day he would kill. Even those at school with him said he was a misfit, a "quiet boy with an alarming temper". He took his temper out on smaller boys. As a child, he wandered the streets looking for dogs and cats to torture – strapping bangers to them to blow them up or set them on fire. He was described by many as an attention seeker. Huntley is known to have taken several overdoses of prescription drugs, and tried to kill himself at least three times.

Huntley was advised by his lawyers not long after the trial that he would never leave prison. He joined a list of murderers who would never be freed, including the late Harold Shipman, John Duffy and Roy Whiting, responsible for the murder of Sarah Payne. The Criminal Justice Act, which came into force 12 hours after Huntley was convicted, meant the ultimate power to determining how long killers stay in prison rests with the Lord Chief Justice rather than the Home Secretary.

Between 2004 and 2006 Huntley tried on two separate occasions to overdose. He was found with vile child porn in his cell in 2006, one month after his latest suicide bid, hidden on a CD disguised as a music album. It was thought that the "album" was given to the convicted killer by freed child rapist Billy Blower, who was informed on by a disgusted relative. The material, thought to contain audio recordings of kids being abused, was thought to have been passed among some of the 570 inmates at Wakefield prison – most of them child sex offenders.

Later that same year, psychology tests showed that Huntley was one of the most dangerous and deeply disturbed sex killers being held in Britain's prison system. He was found to be a compulsive liar and schizophrenic psychopath with a degree of abnormal sexual behaviour that was described as "off the scale", even for convicted paedophiles. The test also showed that he was deeply paranoid about being attacked by other prisoners. He was given a score of 98 for dysfunctional sexual behaviour, 94 for paranoia and 92 for psychopathic deviancy. In known sex offenders, 80 is considered an extremely high score. Britain has had a number of notorious and reviled murderers throughout history, but according to many, Ian Huntley is amongst the worst. The fact that he will serve at least 40 years in prison must be little comfort for two grieving families, who faced the nightmare of losing two precious children in a murderous attack at his hands.

Mick Philpott

(2012)

A woman was arrested on 11th May 2012 on suspicion of murdering five children in a horrific house fire in Allenton, Derby. "The youngsters, aged between five and 10, died in the inferno despite father Mick Philpott's desperate attempts to save them," reported the *Mirror*. A sixth child aged 13 was rushed to hospital and was treated in a specialist burns unit. Dad of 17 Philpott, who had appeared on ITV's *Jeremy Kyle Show*, lived in the semi-detached house with wife Mairead (31). Another woman had also been residing with him, but was said to have moved out just before the fire, after becoming tired of the love triangle. The children who died were named as Jade (10), John (nine), Jack (seven), Jesse (six), and Jayden (five). The woman, aged 28, was being held by police on suspicion of their murder. Later, a man aged 38 from Derby was also arrested in connection with the deaths.

Neighbours called firefighters at around 3.45am when they saw the front door in flames. The blaze quickly engulfed the first floor, where the children were asleep in their bedrooms. Neighbour Daniel Stevenson (23) said: "I woke up in the middle of the night and heard Mick shouting in his garden. I opened the window and could smell smoke. Mick was absolutely frantic, screaming about his kids.

"I woke my brother Callum and he ran outside and round to the back of the house. I called the fire brigade as I could see smoke pouring out of the windows. My brother grabbed a ladder and started climbing up to reach the windows at the back of the house – there was no sign of Mick's wife or the children, though. He managed to smash a window but the police arrived within minutes and stopped him.

"Mick was distraught. There was nothing he could do to get to his kids. I don't know how he got out, but the fire seemed to be burning from the front."

Paramedics were seen trying to revive the children outside the house. Sean Frame, of Derby Fire and Rescue, said: "The crews worked extremely hard in very difficult circumstances and very quickly located six casualties. They removed them to open air and worked with paramedics to try to resuscitate them." But only Duwayne (13) survived the scene and was rushed to the burns unit at Birmingham Children's Hospital. He was said to be in a critical condition. A floral tribute left at the scene read: "Such beautiful children, so cruelly taken. We will miss you so much." All five youngsters went to St George's Catholic Primary School in Littleover. The tragedy happened on the same day that Philpott (55) was due in court over a matter thought to relate to custody of his children. He had previously hit the headlines for demanding a larger council house after getting his wife and another woman pregnant at the same time. He claimed he could not look after the two women and children properly because they were crammed into a three-bedroom semi. The council said the home where the family lived was the biggest they had available. Speaking in the past about his unusual home life Mick said: "What man wouldn't want two women?" He also featured on television, where he had several angry exchanges with Jeremy Kyle. However, just before the fire, Philpott's family life was breaking down. The woman who moved out was thought to have taken her five children away from the family home following the couple's split. One neighbour said: "Mick was very, very upset. He was brilliant with the kids and devoted to them. He had already been to court to try to get custody and the judgment was expected today. He was confident of getting them back. What happened is really shocking." That same day, Philpott wrote on Facebook: "I love all my children more than life itself including the ones who are not my flesh and blood."

Duwayne died in hospital two days later after Philpott and his wife Mairead took the decision to switch off his life support machine. With six deaths in the family, stepbrother Mikey Philpott (14) said: "It's tearing us to pieces that they have gone just like that. It's been really hard to take it all in ... I'd like justice for my brothers and sisters more than anything – it is strung out that someone can just do something like that." He continued: "I was pretty close to all my brothers and sisters. I didn't realize how close until I lost them. Duwayne was a great brother. I spent a lot of time fishing with him at weekends. Jade was a proper daddy's girl, always smiling. You could never get John to shut up, bless him. He was really playful. Then there was Jesse. You couldn't get five minutes alone without her, she was always clinging on to your leg.

"It was the same with Jayden. Jack was like me, a proper computer nerd, always on his Nintendo DS. They were a lovely bunch, I really miss them. They were like my best friends, always there for me and keeping a smile on my face." He added: "I am in touch with my other brothers and sisters, we are sending little updates and messages asking how we are all doing. I talk to my dad when I can."

Former baker Philpott had 17 children by five different women. On Duwayne's death, he and Mairead decided that the boy's organs would be donated in the hope that other children could be saved. Post mortem examinations revealed that five of the children died from the effects of smoke inhalation. Meanwhile, emergency services told how Philpott made "valiant" attempts to rescue his children. After 24 hours, the woman and man in police custody were released without charge.

Police said that forensic tests suggested the blaze "was not accidental and initial indications [are] that it was deliberately set". A reward of £3,500 was offered by local businessmen for any information leading to a conviction in the case.

On 16th May, Philpott wept as he told of the house fire that killed six of his children. He was speaking publicly for the first time since the tragedy, backing a police appeal for the killer to give him- or herself up. He cried as he expressed his thanks to all those who had tried to help. He sobbed: "First of all, I want to thank my three eldest children because they have helped us cope with what's going on. And then there's a young lad who tried to get in the house the same as myself and, of course, all the emergency services and the doctors and nurses. We grew up in a community that's had a lot of problems with violence and God knows what else. But to see them come together like they have is just overwhelming." He continued: "Those poor gentlemen from the fire brigade who saw what we've seen – my heart goes out to them. It's not just us who are suffering, it's them too, it's everybody."

Police then confirmed that the fire was started deliberately by someone pouring petrol through the letterbox. The youngsters were overcome by fumes upstairs in the house, while Philpott and his wife slept downstairs. They were woken by the smoke alarm. One theory at the time was that the arsonist may have held a grudge because of Philpott's "celebrity status" as a "superdad", and police were investigating reports of threats against him on Facebook. What nobody knew – except those involved – was that it was Philpott himself who was responsible for the deaths of his six children.

One neighbour said: "Mick is an amazing family man. He loved all those kids to bits and this will break him." But it didn't take police long to start piecing the story together, and by 23rd May, a caravan and minibus belonging to the children's parents were being examined by experts. The vehicles were taken away from the charred home as the investigation continued into the death of the children a fortnight earlier. Derbyshire Assistant Chief Constable Steve Cotterill said: "The vehicles are being examined at a garage. We are still keeping an open mind as to the reasons for the fire being set." It was thought that the Philpotts used the caravan as extra accommodation to sleep in and that the minibus was used to take the children to and from school. The couple sobbed their hearts out on TV after the tragic deaths, but just two weeks later, Mick Philpott and wife Mairead were charged with six counts of murder after being quizzed separately for 35 hours by detectives.

Assistant Chief Constable Steve Cotterill revealed he had received "important information" from members of the public. But he added: "I want to stress that the two charges this evening should not be seen as the end of the investigation. We are determined to get to the truth of what happened and still want people to tell us what they know about this tragedy." The Crown Prosecution Service said on 30th May that there was "sufficient evidence" for the case to go to court: the pair were to appear before Southern Derbyshire magistrates the following day. The press then reported that the couple had shared their home with Philpott's mistress, Lisa Willis (28), but in February 2012 she moved out with five of her and Mick's children after a row. Lisa and her brother-in-law were arrested on suspicion of murder just days after the blaze, but later freed without charge.

Lisa had provided police with an alibi.

The accused couple applied for compassionate leave from custody to attend the funerals of their six murdered children, but the Prison Service said that any application would be "subject to a strict risk assessment where public protection was key". The result of this was that both parents were banned from attending. There were fears for the couple's safety, as there had been angry outbursts from the public gallery when they appeared in court the month before. By 13th June, the bodies were released by the coroner so the funerals could go ahead. On 20th June, a third person was arrested over the children's deaths. A 45-year-old man was questioned by detectives while forensic experts searched an address in Derby. Sources said the new suspect was not related to Philpott; he was arrested just two days before the funerals of the children were due to take place.

Murder charges were dropped in December 2012, and it was announced that the couple were to face charges of manslaughter at a trial to be held in February 2013. The couple entered their pleas to six counts of manslaughter at Birmingham Crown Court. Paul Mosley, the third person arrested, from Derby, also pleaded not guilty to manslaughter.

On 12th February 2013, the *Mirror* reported: "Twisted Mick Philpott ended up killing six of his children in a house fire after hatching a sick plot to get revenge on an ex-lover ..." He planned to torch his home, then blame the arson attack on former mistress Lisa Willis, who was fighting him for custody of four other youngsters, jurors were told. Philpott allegedly told friends: "She won't get away with this ... watch this space." He was said to have sown the seeds of his "evil plan" by claiming to police that Lisa had made threats against himself and the children. No one was supposed to get hurt in the blaze, the court heard. Philpott and Mairead, together with family friend Mosley, had arranged an elaborate rescue to make them appear innocent victims. But it all went horribly wrong when the early morning blaze tore out of control through the house, trapping the six children. The court was told that the inferno, started by petrol in the hallway, was so fierce it melted the front door. As the bodies of the children were carried outside by police, Philpott ran forward and had to be restrained. The jury of six men and six women was played a recording of the harrowing 999 call by Mairead just minutes after the fire took hold. Philpott leapt to his feet and tried to leave the dock, shouting: "I can't listen to it!" After being restrained by court officers, he sat with his head bowed and his hands covering his ears. In the recording Mairead said: "I can't get to my kids." The operator asked: "How many?" Mairead replied: "There are six of them." Then Philpott was heard yelling: "I can't get in the window. Smoke's everywhere." Mairead said: "Oh my God, please. He just smashed the bedroom window and there is smoke coming from everywhere." On the recording Philpott could be heard yelling that the children were all in the back bedroom. They were, in fact, found in three separate bedrooms. Prosecutor Richard Latham, QC, suggested that Philpott had expected them all to be in the same room "as part of the rescue plan". Philpott was secretly taped by police at a hotel following the blaze. He allegedly told Mairead: "Make sure you stick to the story." A nurse also allegedly overheard him saying to a male friend: "It was not meant to end like this." Mr Latham said: "What is alleged is that these children died as a result of the unlawful acts of these defendants who were acting together in a joint enterprise."

Jurors were then shown plans of the house in Victory Road, Allenton, Derby. Philpott was said to be furious when his lover moved out. Mairead slept in either the conservatory or the living room while Philpott and Lisa slept in the caravan. Lisa had begun a sexual relationship with the married man when she was aged around 17 or 18. Philpott, claimed Mr Latham, had total control over his mistress. Even her wages from a cleaning job were paid directly into his bank account, as were her benefits. Jurors were told that Philpott had a sexual relationship with both women, but often said he was unhappy with his wife: he said he wanted to divorce Mairead so he could marry Lisa, but wanted to keep both women under the same roof. Jurors were told that the "catalyst" to the tragedy was Lisa's decision that she didn't want to live with Philpott any longer, because of his violence and bullying. Philpott, meanwhile, complained that he had lost £1,000 a month in child benefit when she left. Mr

Latham said: "She stood up to him, he was no longer in control and that was absolutely unacceptable to him." The Philpotts and Mosley still denied six counts of manslaughter.

The court heard on 14th February about the "nightmare" life that Philpott's ex-girlfriend Heather Kehoe (22) had with him during a four-year relationship. She met Philpott when she was 14 years old and began sleeping with him at 15. Ms Kehoe said he later attacked her in their home, and the violence got worse as time went on. She added: "It was a bit of a whirlwind. Mick was like a Jekyll and Hyde character. He had that caring side. He knew what to say to make me feel special.

"Everything had to be his way. I soon learned what his way was. He was violent. He would hit me or lash out. But I always thought that the mental abuse was the worst. He played mind games." Philpott's then wife, Pamela Lomax, caught the couple in bed together at the marital home and threw them both out in early 1996. The pair ran away to Derby and eventually moved into the house in Victory Road where the fire took place. Kehoe said that Philpott was violent towards her within weeks, when she complained she was homesick, and twice pinned her to the floor of the living room, the second time when she was pregnant. The couple went on to have two sons, Mikey, in his late teens at the time of the trial, and Aidan, a year younger. Their relationship worsened because she could not give birth to the daughter for whom Philpott longed.

"He wanted a girl," she said. "He used to beat me for that.

It was my fault Aidan was not a girl. He wanted lots of children and to be the one to stop at home and look after them. He wanted 11 children. He said something about a football team and reserves." Prosecutor Richard Latham asked her: "Did you make a decision about this football team?" Ms Kehoe replied: "I decided it was not happening." She began using contraception, which only made Philpott's violence towards her worse. She said their relationship ended in 2000 after Philpott ordered Mikey, then a toddler, to hit her during a blazing row. The court was told the terrifying bust-up began after she made a remark about Mikey being "my son too". She sobbed: "It started verbally but it became physical. He was trying to eject me from the back door into the back garden. I tried to resist. He shouted Mikey over and told him to punch me in the face and to kick me and call me names." Asked if Mikey did that, she replied: "He did."

Before Ms Kehoe gave evidence, Philpott's former mistress described his wife Mairead as a "perfect mum". Lisa Willis said the pair were like "sisters" even though they were bedding Philpott on alternate nights. Giving evidence from behind a screen for a second day, she agreed with Mairead's defence barrister Shaun Smith that the kids were "well-fed, happy children" who "loved going to school and loved being at home". Ms Willis also agreed that Mairead would "never harm a hair on the head of any child, let alone her own". Asked by Mr Smith if Mairead had a "bad bone in her body", she replied: "No."

Philpott was overheard on his mobile saying: "he's going to drop us in it" a week after the six children died. He was alleged to have made the remark at the Royal Derby Hospital, where his wife was a cleaner. Claire Tyler, who worked with Mairead, told jurors that Philpott had asked her if there were any security people around and put his hood up before disappearing briefly. When he returned, she said he "stood back" to receive a call on his mobile. She admitted under cross-examination that she didn't know who Philpott was talking to, but she also described how Mairead, "a lovely bubbly person", instantly became quiet whenever her husband was around. Her character was said to have changed in 2011 following an abortion.

The court then heard how Lisa Willis had moved out of Philpott's home to move in with Ian Cousins, her brother-in-law. Philpott had then accused Cousins of having an affair with his ex-mistress. Cousins told the court he was not affected by Philpott's claims about the affair on Facebook, which he insisted were "untrue". He added: "It was like a pinch of salt. Me, Lisa and Amanda [his wife] knew it wasn't true." He then denied that he had been involved in setting the fire. Anthony Orchard, QC, defending, asked: "Do you have any direct knowledge of who set this fire?" Cousins replied: "No." In the end Lisa had moved out of Cousins' home to live in a refuge.

By now, the jury were aware that prosecutors believed Philpott, Mairead and Mosley set the fire in a botched plan to frame Lisa. The court heard how a month before the fire Philpott was driving relatives of darts star Colin Osborne to a match in his minibus. He took a call from his wife, and said: "Sorry, guys, that was my missus. My ex is threatening to petrol bomb the house." Osborne's wife, Sarah, told the court: "I just heard him say, 'Call me if you get any more.' Then he turned around and said: 'Sorry guys, someone has just called threatening to torch the house with the kids inside.'"

It then transpired that Philpott had bought cannabis and Mairead was "stoned" hours before the blaze. Neighbour Adam Taylor said that as they went to a local drug dealer Philpott voiced fears that he might lose the next day's custody fight with Lisa. Mr Taylor said he was "paranoid" he wouldn't win.

On 26th February, jurors heard how Philpott "staged a pretend faint when he saw their bodies for the first time in the mortuary…" He also asked for booze and engaged in horseplay with a police liaison officer days after the tragedy while bemused staff looked on, the court was told by Marie Smith, the mortuary boss, who said that Philpott referred to the young victims as "little shits" (although she thought this was probably meant as a term of endearment) and described the couple's visits as a "circus". In the witness box she said how Philpott had asked for all the children to be in the room together for the couple's first visit, four days after they died. She left them alone, and then heard Mairead shout out Philpott's name. Ms Smith returned to the room and spotted him on the floor. She said: "He appeared to have fainted. He was lying in a very restricted area, about two-and-a-half feet of floor. But the children's sheets were not disturbed in any way. There was no sign of him disturbing anything. He appeared to be lying in the recovery position. His hand was under his chin. It looked very unlikely to me that it was a genuine faint. In my experience as a mortuary manager, having seen many friends and relatives faint for whatever reason, it did not appear to be genuine. He did not wake up, so I asked a member of staff to get some water and call a doctor. He immediately woke up and got up when I said I was going to get a doctor."

The Philpotts visited the mortuary three times in the days following their children's horrific deaths. Ms Smith said the couple were accompanied by up to a dozen other people at times. On one occasion she and another member of staff saw Philpott messing about with a police officer in the morgue. She added: "It appeared like there was a lot of horseplay going on. Not the family liaison officer, just Mick Philpott. He was bending forward and pulling his sweatshirt up and tapping his back. Then he grabbed the family liaison officer in a headlock." Ms Smith told how he was later offered a glass of water and asked if he could have a gin in it. She said that no relative had ever asked that before. She said the accused's behaviour during his visits "wasn't fitting with what had taken place with the children" and believed it was "irrational". While at the mortuary Philpott had angrily demanded that police find those responsible for killing the innocent youngsters. He also "issued acts of revenge" against the person he claimed had started the fire. Smith said: "He would be quite angry one minute, then be apologizing the next, but it did not seem genuine." Social worker Nicola Atterbury told the court that Philpott appeared to fake his distress during a meeting she had with him and his wife after the tragedy. She added: "I thought at one point he was going to cry, it was almost child-like, he was squeezing his face as a child would to produce tears."

In the days following the blaze, Philpott flirted with a blonde WPC and invited her to his hotel room. He called officer Joanne Halford "gorgeous", and she felt "uncomfortable" as Philpott "joked" about the tragedy. He allegedly told the officer he was "cross" with his wife for telling police that they enjoyed "threesomes".

In early March, the jury heard how the blaze "roared" through the children's home. Fire investigator Mat Lee described the terrifying noise the inferno would have made as it spread through the house. He told the court it was started in the downstairs hallway close to the front door when petrol was deliberately ignited. He said: "I would best describe it as a well-stoked chimney fire, cracking, popping and roaring." It was then announced to the court that Philpott's boxer shorts had traces of petrol on them. An investigator said the Shell fuel – also found on the 56-year-old's right training shoe – was the same type as was discovered at the seat of the blaze at the council house. Forensic expert Rebecca Jewell told the jury:

"We can tell unequivocally which brand the fuel has come from by their additives."

Mick Philpott broke down in the witness box on 13th March as he tearfully denied starting the blaze. He told the court that he played no part in the fire, and appeared to collapse as a tape of the 999 call was played. His barrister, Anthony Orchard, asked him if he had set the fire. Philpott replied: "No." He added that he did not know who torched the family home, but when asked if he had suspicions said: "I do." He then gave his version of events.

Philpott said he was woken up by a smoke alarm in the early hours of 11th May 2012 and saw bright light and thick smoke. He said his first thought was for his kids. He dressed, ran outside and put a ladder up to a window and tried to break the glass with a child's tennis racket, but was unsuccessful. Eventually he smashed the window with a socket set, but could not climb inside. Philpott admitted having a "big gob" and said he split public opinion: "I live my life the way I want to … people either love me or hate me." He told the jury he regretted appearing on the *Jeremy Kyle Show* with Mairead and Lisa in 2006, because his children were later bullied and threatened. He insisted he was a good father and denied claims he stopped Mairead and Lisa going out; but he admitted hitting both women after they allegedly hit Jade. He admitted that the night of the fire he had been "kissing and cuddling" Mairead as she performed a sex act on Mosley. He also admitted going dogging with Mairead both before and after the blaze, and that they had smoked cannabis together.

Philpott claimed that the petrol found on his clothes was because he hadn't had a bath for three months. The jury heard that his children branded him "a tramp" because of his lack of personal hygiene. He was known to have worn the same boxers and jogging bottoms for days, and said petrol could have spilt on his clothes when he lent his neighbour a strimmer. He told the court that the family bathroom was being renovated. The prosecution, however, advised him that his wife was no longer sticking to the "cover-up" story and had "broken ranks". Mr Latham also accused Philpott of resorting to "crocodile tears" and of flopping to the ground, or throwing a "sicky", which the prosecutor claimed was "an act". Shaun Smith, defending Mairead, told the accused man: "You regarded Mairead as your property, your slave. She did everything even when you were having a relationship with another woman. You think you own her."

On 15th March the court heard how Philpott started the "nightmare" fire that killed his six children because he wanted to be a "hero" and rescue them. But the blaze got "bigger than he ever expected". As Mr Latham cross-examined Philpott for a second day, he accused him of placing a ladder at the back of the house so he could rescue the children after he lit the fire. But the plan backfired because the bedroom window was closed, trapping the children inside.

Paul Mosley decided to exercise "his right to silence", and chose not to testify in his defence.

After Philpott was convicted of six counts of manslaughter on 2nd April 2013, he clutched his St Christopher and kissed it six times. But his "pious" gesture was accompanied by a sneering remark to a detective in the court: "Wanker, it's not over yet." Arrogant Philpott hit out after he, Mairead and Mosley were convicted of killing the children. Despite knowing he was facing life in jail, callous Philpott blew a kiss to daughter Michaela, who was sitting nearby. Even with the overwhelming evidence stacked against them, the trio kept up their shocking pretence that the fire was the work of Lisa Willis. The jury, however, saw through the twisted lies – and even family members believed them to be guilty. After the manslaughter verdicts were read out by the jury foreman, Mairead's sister, Bernadette Duffy, screamed from the public gallery: "You murdering bastards. I knew you'd done it from day one." Dawn Bestwick, Philpott's sister, said: "Following today's verdict we believe justice has been served … We have listened objectively to all the evidence in this trial to understand what happened to our six beautiful children. This past year has been a very difficult time for our family as we have had to come to terms with what Michael, Mairead and Paul Mosley have done."

It transpired that following the fire there were times when Philpott acted as if nothing had happened. The *Mirror* wrote: "Apart from a shameful display of crocodile tears alongside

Mairead at a police press conference, the warped dad showed little emotion. One night he even sang the Elvis hit 'Suspicious Minds' at a karaoke night – just days after killing his children. Drinkers at his local pub, the Navigation, looked on stunned as he belted out the song while Mairead sat giggling nearby. Wearing a Stetson hat and seemingly without a care in the world, Philpott believed he had got away with the crime."

One drinker said: "People were looking at each other. They couldn't believe what they were seeing and hearing. He was loving the attention." Just hours later Philpott attended a church service for his dead children. The *Mirror* continued: "Astonishingly, he laughed and joked with onlookers as prayers were said for his children inside." A church worker said: "His reaction to the deaths was nowhere near normal. He was there with a big fat smile on his face."

Pictures of the fire's devastation were released following the trial. They showed that the home was left a charred mess. They showed the blackened bedroom the children died in. Unknown to the Philpotts, the police bugged their Premier Inn hotel room, where they stayed after being made homeless by the fire. Detectives listened in disbelief as Mairead performed a sex act on Mosley in Philpott's presence. Her husband was heard to whisper to her: "We are sticking to the story. I didn't mean to do it, on my life." The *Mirror* reported that the couple got stoned on powerful skunk cannabis and had regular sex sessions, and revealed that the "sickening couple" spoke about profiting from their children's deaths. Philpott targeted a fund set up by kind-hearted locals – seeing it as a way to "getting rich quick". Sympathetic members of the public raised more than £15,000 to pay for the funeral service, and Philpott demanded that fund bosses – who included Mosley – should give left-over money to his family in Argos vouchers. He also ordered friends to sell teddy bears left outside the scene on eBay – with all profits going to him. One trustee said: "At first, it was to pay for the funerals and to give money to the Philpotts who had lost everything. People soon realized the way the wind was blowing and not a penny went to them." Service official Samantha Shallow described the case as "harrowing and challenging".

Assistant Chief Constable Steve Cotterill said the killing of the six children was an "evil, stupid, shameful act". He branded Philpott, Mairead and Mosley as "devious liars" who displayed no remorse whatsoever. He said that Philpott did nothing to save his children, and continued: "Any parent would have paid the ultimate sacrifice trying to save their kids in that fire. Mick Philpott didn't." He said the only missing piece of the jigsaw was what exactly happened, but he stated: "I firmly believe all three of them were part and parcel of that plot. It was an evil, stupid, shameful act. I will never be able to forgive them for that, understand that or have sympathy for them. This has been the saddest most tragic case I have ever dealt with. I have become extremely angry at the needless loss of life. There are six little kids that have not got the chance to grow up."

Detectives were suspicious of the Philpotts within 24 hours of the blaze. The Derbyshire Police chief said: "The fire was set behind the front door, and coincidentally the fire happened on the same day of the child custody court date. We were getting no reports of anyone acting suspiciously outside the property and there had been no arsons of that type for months. It started to ring alarm bells." Mr Cotterill met the couple once at a press conference five days after the tragedy, and was astonished by the "supposedly grieving" father's attitude. He described Philpott as in "quite a jovial manner, like an excited child".

More about Philpott's past came to light following the trial, when Heather Kehoe spoke to the newspapers about how she became his terrified sex slave while still in her mid-teens. She said he began grooming her when she was just 13 years old and started plying her with cigarettes and alcohol. His appalling abuse didn't only include horrific daily beatings, but also his alleged rape of her at knifepoint when she was pregnant with Mikey. She said Philpott forced her to become a five-times-a-day sex slave and threatened to kill one of their sons when he was just a week old. Ms Kehoe had been banned by the judge from revealing what her life had really been like with Philpott until after the trial. It was her evidence that helped convict Philpott of six killings.

She said: "It was hell on earth. I'd get beaten for anything." Heather added that Philpott would abuse her as he listened to a song, 'Kim', by rapper Eminem, about someone planning to murder an estranged wife. She often knew hours before a beating that it was coming because he would play the song. It was the soundtrack to his mental and physical abuse. Philpott had, in fact, tried to kill his 17-year-old ex-fiancée Kim Hill by stabbing her 27 times. He also turned the knife on Kim's mother, and was jailed for seven years at the age of 21 after being convicted in 1978 of attempted murder and grievous bodily harm with intent. A week after Aidan was born, Philpott held a pillow over his face and told Heather that if she ever did anything wrong again she could "kiss goodbye" to the baby. Heather eventually turned her back on her middle-class parents – who were horrified at their daughter's relationship with a much older married man – but she found life in Derby horrendous. She waited "hand and foot" on perverted Philpott while he got stoned, watched TV and abused her. Her wages from her job as a cleaner at East Midlands Airport were paid directly into his bank account. The terrified 16-year-old, meanwhile, was forced to live on a pittance. She said: "I wasn't allowed any sleep because I had to make up for not having been there during the day. I would arrive home at night after a 16-hour shift, then cook a meal and do all the housework. Rolling his fags became another task of mine. If I forgot to do them the night before, he'd make me get up an hour early to do them. Things got very nasty, very quickly." It was after Mikey was ordered to abuse his mother that Heather found the courage and the strength to leave Philpott. She described how Philpott backhanded her hard across the face; he had hold of her hair as he kicked and punched her. Then he told Mikey to tell "Mummy what a naughty bitch she was". Philpott then kicked her again and punched her in front of her son. Mikey punched her in the face and tried to kick her in the stomach. "Something snapped inside me and I thought, I can't do this any more, I need to get away and get the kids away from that man." After leaving Philpott, Heather had a nine-month legal battle before she finally won custody of her children. She then had a long fight with him over access.

After the fire a woman came forward claiming that Philpott raped her in a "squalid caravan" in his front garden in 2005. The victim told detectives that the killer spiked her cup of tea before attacking her. She kept quiet about the alleged attack before breaking down and telling police in 2012. The woman, who could not be named for legal reasons, said: "It was rape. He makes my flesh crawl." She made a videotaped statement, but police decided to wait until the outcome of the trial before quizzing Philpott about the attack. The woman was often at the Philpotts' home, and when he got up in the afternoon it was usual for her to take him a cup of tea. She broke down and made a separate statement to police after they interviewed her about the fire. She added: "Mick's evil. He's a child-killer … it's all about Mick. He wants what he wants and will stop at nothing to get it. He's always been the same. He deserves everything that's coming to him. He's hard and he's tough … but there's plenty of lifers who are harder and tougher."

Victim three was Kim Hill, who was left fighting for her life after Philpott stabbed her in a frenzied knife attack after she dumped him. The girl was just 17 when he crept into her home in the middle of the night and launched his attack. He told her: "If I can't have you, no one else will." Kim said she would never forget Philpott's eyes as he stabbed her. Prosecutors in the case against Philpott compared the bloody attack with the blaze, and wanted to show in court what the man was capable of when he didn't get his own way. However, the judge, Mrs Justice Thirlwell, ruled the jury should not be told of the previous conviction because it happened 35 years before. After the trial, Kim revealed how Philpott was furious that she wanted to end their three-year relationship. She recalled: "He came into my bedroom and put his hand on my face and told me to be quiet ... He said something and then I thought he started punching me. I couldn't walk and then I just fell on the floor and he was attacking me again. The next thing I knew I was in hospital over a week later." As Kim's mother, Shirley, tried to intervene and call the police, she too was stabbed. Kim "died" twice in the ambulance and on the operating table as surgeons battled to save her life. She spent over six weeks in intensive care and still bears the scars all over her body. Her horrific ordeal left her severely traumatized and 35 years later she still received counselling. Philpott slit her stomach open and cut her all down her back, on the tops of her legs and on her arms. He punctured both Kim's lungs and went through her liver and kidney. During the trial, Philpott claimed he could not remember attacking either woman, but admitted to going to the girl's house to persuade her to take him back. Jailing Philpott for seven years, Mr Justice Pain described him as a "dangerous young man". He said: "These are extremely serious matters and you are obviously, despite your youth, a dangerous man. It is necessary … you are in custody for a fairly long time." Kim also revealed how Philpott was arrested for having sex with a minor and was jailed after being caught with her.

The *Mirror* said: "They epitomised everything about the 'Jeremy Kyle' generation". Mick Philpott, a self-confessed scrounger who raked in £38,000 a year in benefit claims, and Mairead, a mum of six who happily shared her run-down council house with her husband's young mistress. The article continued: "Their bizarre lifestyle made them celebrities of a sort – culminating in their obligatory appearance on Kyle's ITV show in 2007. Philpott grinned with pride as the star of the show was billed: 'Father to 15 … wife and girlfriend pregnant again!' Outraging the audience, he bragged: 'What man wouldn't want two women? I've never worn a condom. They spoil sex.'" He had come to public attention the year before when his demands for a bigger house prompted a backlash in which he was dubbed "Britain's Biggest Scrounger" and "Shameless Mick", which also led to him appearing on *This Morning* and a documentary: *Ann Widdecombe Versus the Benefit Culture*. In a *Mirror* interview in his home in 2007, smug Philpott said he was "a lucky man".

In April 2013, with friends and relatives still reeling in shock at the deaths of six innocent children, Philpott penned a letter to a friend. There were no words of remorse or regret. Instead the depraved killer spilled out his lurid thoughts about Mairead, displayed a deluded belief that they would be freed and spoke of a grasping plan to sue the police who arrested him. He told Mick Russell that as soon as he was released he wanted to get drunk and have sex with his wife at the graves of the children. His friend also revealed how Philpott had described his daughter as a "golliwog" after seeing her charred corpse and boasted about a sleazy sex session with his wife. Philpott wrote in the rambling four-page letter: "But me and my darling beloved wife, the most important thing that we will do when this happens is to spend the whole day with our babies, at the graveside. We don't care if it's raining, gale force winds, snowing, I'm going straight up there. Then we shall probably, no, we will, rape each other ... then we can all celebrate our freedom as long as they get the bastards." The envelope he used was garishly decorated in peach and black pen with the names of his dead children set in hearts on the back. He had written: "We love you". But Mick Russell said that Philpott showed none of this love when he visited the mortuary. He had accompanied Philpott to the hospital to identify the bodies, and the father had just joked his way around. On the same page as the article describing the letter was a piece that revealed Philpott was on bail awaiting trial for a road rage attack at the time of the fire. He had been in court a week before the tragic night, and admitted common assault but denied dangerous driving. He punched Jonathan Welham (42), whose daughter was with him, after becoming convinced that the driver had pulled out in front of him at a roundabout.

Mick Russell described how Jack, aged three, on one occasion was making a noise while Philpott was on the phone, and his father drop-kicked him across the room. Sharon Russell was also sickened by the actions of the couple following the deaths. She said: "I remember Mairead excitedly showing me a black dress she had bought for the funeral. As soon as I saw it I said to her, 'You can't wear that.' It was long at the back but cut so short at the front that it barely covered her underwear and the front was see-through lace. She seemed surprised by my reaction and said, 'Oh well, I can wear it to the after-party.' What sort of person talks about a party after their children's funeral?" Mick and Sharon Russell were deceived by Philpott's lies and felt betrayed by their former friend's behaviour. Mr Russell said: "I just can't believe how he's conned me. I am embarrassed I ever stood up for him."

Philpott was jailed for life in April 2013. The defiant convicted killer flicked a V-sign at the public gallery and grinned at police as he swaggered out of the dock to begin his sentence. However, there was fury over the length of the trio's sentences. Philpott's sister, Dawn Bestwick, slammed the jail terms as a "pittance". Philpott was given life, meaning he could be out in 15 years; Mairead and Mosley were given 17 years each, meaning they could be out in just eight and a half years. Philpott was described by the judge as "disturbingly dangerous" and Mrs Justice Thirlwell also told the court that he was the "driving force behind the defendants' arson plot". She also told Philpott that he had no moral compass and said: "It is, in my judgment, a uniquely grave set of offences." She said she accepted that they did not plan to kill the children, but intended to put them through a terrifying ordeal. She said that "It was wicked and dangerous" and added that Philpott might never be released from prison. Philpott and Mosley were taken to Wakefield prison while Mairead was taken to New Hall jail. None of the killers had shown any remorse.

In November 2013, Mairead Philpott failed to have her 17-year sentence cut on appeal. Carole Malone wrote: "It took six children to die before the law finally got the measure of Mick Philpott ... of his evil, his greed, his immorality. And now that we have there need be no more lies. No more pretence. No more of his fake rants about how much he loved his kids and how he'd die for them if he had to. Because Mick Philpott had the chance to die for his children. And he didn't. This callous, cold-blooded killer stood outside the house he'd deliberately set alight and watched while others risked THEIR lives to save them. But they couldn't be saved and one by one their blackened little bodies were dragged out of that house ... killed because of their father's greed. This monster gambled with their lives for money ... and lost. More importantly THEY lost because they had a father possessed with the unshakeable belief that anything he wanted he HAD to have. And what he wanted was money and revenge on the lover who'd left him. And to get it he was prepared to risk the lives of those children he kept telling us he loved. Mick Philpott is a grotesque tale of our time. A man who wasn't just allowed to live lavishly off the state, but to publicly brag about it ... But the truth – as hideous and uncomfortable as it is – is that if this man hadn't been obsessed about recovering the £1,000 a month he'd lost in benefits when lover Lisa walked out with five of their kids, then Duwayne, Jade, John, Jack, Jesse and Jayden would still be alive today. They'd never have been used as live bait in his sickening game of greed and revenge. It is also the truth that ALL of Philpott's children owe their existence to the fact that their father saw the benefit system as his own personal bank. The more children he had, the more money he got to spend on booze and cannabis. Nothing can bring back those poor dead children but it's to be hoped that in prison Mick Philpott feels just a fraction of the fear they must have felt that terrible night when they realized there was no escape. Because if ever there was a man who deserves to know what hell is like it's him, a man who justified the way he lived by insisting that, above all else, he loved his kids. That's what he kept telling the world and tragically for those children, the world believed him. But Mick Philpott didn't give a damn about his children.

It was always about him. Which is why, however much we pray he is tortured by their deaths, the truth is that the loss of them means nothing to him."

Dale Cregan

(2012)

On 12th August 2012, police were questioning one suspect and hunting another after two gun and grenade attacks killed a man. David Short (46) died from bullet and blast injuries in the first incident in Manchester. It took place just a couple of months after his son Mark (23) had been shot dead in a pub in the city. Greater Manchester Police confirmed that a 37-year-old man had been arrested on suspicion of murder, relating to the attack in Clayton and the second attack minutes later in Droylsden.

Police responded to reports of gunfire at a home, and said an explosion there was caused by a grenade. Shots were then fired at a second property two miles away, where detectives said there was another blast. Nobody was injured in this second incident. Police then searched for 29-year-old Dale Cregan for questioning over the two incidents and also the murder of Mark Short. Assistant Chief Constable Garry Shewan said: "We have dedicated a significant amount of officers to identify those involved in the attacks and to carry out intensive patrols in the area. Our main priority is finding Dale Cregan so we can arrest him and speak to him about these incidents."

After his son had been murdered, David Short and his family released a statement saying he had been "taken away by cowards". Father of one Mark, an amateur boxer, was shot in the neck at the Cotton Tree pub in Droylsden after masked gunmen walked in and opened fire. Luke Livesey (27), from Hattersley, and Damien Gorman (38), from Glossop, were charged with Mark's murder and with three counts of attempted murder. Mathew James (32) was also charged with murder and three counts of attempted murder, in August 2012.

"Shocking CCTV footage showed two men approaching a property around 10.30am. One of them then casually threw what appeared to be a grenade into the front of a house. Smoke is seen billowing into the street as the two men fled the scene. Luckily no one was hurt in this incident in Droylsden. Mr Shewan confirmed that the police were still searching for Cregan – who was wanted in connection with Mr Short's murder and that of his son, Mark," wrote the *Mirror*.

By 28th August, the reward for the capture of the two fugitives, Cregan and Anthony Wilkinson (33), suspected of killing Mr Short doubled to £50,000. Police said it was the largest sum they had ever offered for information. Meanwhile, Jermaine Ward (24), arrested in connection with Mr Short's murder, was due in court.

On 18th September 2012 a senior officer slammed the deaths of two policewomen as "an act of cold-blooded murder". Greater Manchester Chief Constable Sir Peter Fahy hit out after unarmed WPCs Fiona Bone (32) and Nicola Hughes (23) were brutally shot dead at point-blank range in a hail of

13 bullets – followed by a grenade explosion. He revealed that they might have been deliberately lured to their deaths. He said the "routine" burglary call they had been sent to investigate was bogus – and had been made by their killer. Sir Peter was speaking at a press conference as one-eyed Cregan was under arrest and being questioned over the officers' deaths. As flags flew at half mast over police HQ, he added: "We are all shocked by what happened this morning. We are devastated today by the loss of two of our officers. This is one of the darkest days in the history of the Greater Manchester force, if not for the police service overall, because we have lost two deeply loved and valued colleagues."

Witnesses told how the unsuspecting officers had been approaching the front door of a terraced house in a cul-de-sac in Hattersley, Tameside, shortly before 11.00am when a man stepped out and opened fire. Both women were hit – then the gunman hurled a grenade at their patrol car. Officers who arrived at the scene in Abbey Gardens were in tears after seeing the bloodied bodies of their two colleagues. Fiona had been with the force for five years, Nicola for three. The devastated father of PC Bone said he was "numb with grief". Paul Bone (64) said: "Bring back hanging. Let policemen shoot people on sight. I am just so completely shocked. She was such a lovely girl. I can't even bring myself to think of the wedding."

A short time after the attack, Cregan was arrested after walking into a police station less than three miles away. He had been wanted for questioning for five weeks in connection with the separate gun and grenade attacks. The killings were believed to have been part of a 10-year gangland war, and Cregan had been described as "the most wanted man in Britain". After it emerged that Cregan had been in the area in the days leading up to the murders, even drinking in pubs, one woman told reporters that even though people had seen him, they were all too scared to turn him in no matter how big the reward. Detectives believed members of the public had been harbouring him. Sir Peter said: "It would appear the killer has deliberately done this," and that the motive for the attack was "impossible to fathom", adding: "When they arrived it appears that the gunman emerged into the road and killed these two officers. A firearm was used. A grenade was also used." Armed response units raced to the scene after the shootings, along with an army bomb disposal unit. A fleet of vans and ambulances were parked at the top of the road as a police helicopter hovered overhead. Traffic was blocked from coming on to the estate up to half a mile away. Witnesses told of their horror at the shootings. One said: "I was just waking up when I heard bang, bang, bang, bang. I thought it was just fireworks until there was a bang so loud it was as if somebody had dropped a skip from the sky and it crashed on to the floor."

Leanne Simpson (36), a mother of four, said: "My mum actually heard the shots and she said there was six bangs like a machine gun and then a big boom. She thought it was a firework. I was driving up the road and I saw four policemen running towards me and they were crying." One woman who did not want to be named said her ex-boyfriend saw the shooting. She said: "He was walking back from the doctor's and he heard a shout." He then saw someone come out of the house and shoot the two officers before throwing the grenade. The house where the shootings took place had just been reoccupied after an elderly woman died – and the windows had been covered in whitewash. Police confirmed that a man, believed to be a 32-year-old local barber, and his girlfriend were being questioned as witnesses. Detectives believed they might have been held captive by the killer. David Cameron described the killings as "pure, cold-blooded evil". He added that they were "another reminder of the incredible risks and great work" carried out by the police.

In the hours before she died, Fiona Bone chatted to her fiancé about invitations for their wedding and asked workmates for advice on designing them. A little while later, the dedicated WPC and her colleague Nicola were murdered. The chairman of the Greater Manchester Police Federation, Ian Hanson, said: "I'm going to look beyond uniform here. What we've got are two young girls that went out this morning and they've got an absolute right to come home tonight to their loved ones. This is cold-blooded murder. It's the slaughter of the innocents. I'm struggling to find the words to use to officers out there who've lost friends and colleagues. It's a dark day for policing, it's a dark day for society." Greater Manchester Police officers formed a guard of honour as a private ambulance left the scene. Sir Peter said the women "exemplified the very best of British policing". He said: "Fiona had a great sense of humour – always enjoying a good laugh. She was so happy with her partner and they were in the middle of planning their wedding … Her fellow officers said they loved being partnered with her because she was calm, collected and professional and could defuse situations with her calm gentle way. She was an excellent bobby and cared about her job and the communities that she served." Paying tribute to her colleague, he said: "Nicola enjoyed karate, she was very bubbly and loved life and socializing. She was a chatterbox and always smiling even after a night shift … She was a good listener and couldn't do enough for people." He added: "GMP is in mourning for the loss of two very brave, courageous colleagues."

After the bitter feud that led to the deaths of Mark and David Short, Dale Cregan had become a fugitive in one of Britain's biggest manhunts. His picture, which showed him wearing a black glass eye in his blinded left socket, was circulated nationwide as hundreds of officers were deployed to hunt for him. Detectives carried out 50 raids and armed police patrolled areas that Cregan was known to frequent. They also watched ports and airports in an operation costing millions of pounds. But police believed the man had associates who helped him. It was believed that David Short had been killed in a preemptive strike after he vowed revenge over his son's killing. During the attack at his home in Clayton, his terraced house had been riddled with 9mm bullets and a grenade, thought to be a Soviet-made device. It was believed that David's son Mark's hitman had intended to kneecap him in a punishment attack, but accidentally killed him when the victim crouched down, shooting him in the neck. The Short family had been at loggerheads with rival families for more than 10 years. It was understood that David had been repeatedly warned that his life was in danger, and had taken to wearing a bulletproof vest up to eight years earlier.

Terrorism expert Ben Lopez confirmed that guns, grenades and heavy weapons are illegally trafficked into Britain every day. Lopez, a kidnap rescue consultant, warned that getting weapons on the UK black market was easy. He said: "People in Britain are lulled into a false sense of security because guns are banned here. But they are easily obtained around the world. There are weapons on sale in Africa, the Middle East and America. And after the breakdown of the Eastern Bloc countries, where many weapons got stolen, supply is not an issue. Typically they come in hidden in shipping containers. Look how many drugs come into this country – smuggling heavy weapons is just as easy."

Mr Lopez, who had just published a book, *The Negotiator*, telling of his battle against the kidnap trade, added: "If someone is determined to get their hands on weapons in the UK they will." Despite a total ban on handguns following the Dunblane massacre in 1996, in 2010–11 there were 60 gun killings in England and Wales. At the time, 1.8 million guns were legally held, while there was no reliable estimate for how many illegal weapons there were.

In September 2012, the *Mirror* reported in an exclusive that grenades had become the latest "must have" weapons being sold by underworld arms dealers at knockdown prices. A special investigation found that the terrifying trade was booming. Following the killing of the two WPCs they uncovered a "shocking" array of firepower available on the streets. The death "shopping lists" included guns for hire for as little as £100, to rent or buy, and these black market dealings were said to be worth hundreds of thousands of pounds each year. The paper revealed that high-level criminals were turning to grenades to beef up their armoury, the most commonly used being the Swiss-manufactured British Army-issue L109 and the Yugoslavian-made M75. In the three years to March 2010 there were 14 grenade attacks in the UK – including seven in the North West in just 10 months. Large numbers were thought to have gone missing when the Soviet Union and Yugoslavia split up into smaller states; others were believed to have been stolen from British Army bases. Sources said that it was still mainly "the top boys" who managed to get their hands on the grenades, with young street gangs more likely to make their own terrorist-style devices. One underworld source said: "You can get a grenade for a couple of hundred quid – £250 tops.

It's shocking that something so destructive goes for so little. There's a new pattern emerging. It's about portraying an image of utter violence. It's all about being bigger and badder than your rivals – and having grenades is one step, actually using them takes it even further." The source added that weapons and grenades were often smuggled in from abroad, along with drugs. He said: "A grenade is not the type of thing you stash under a bed or have just lying about. You get one when you need one for a specific purpose."

Meanwhile, the first witnesses on the scene described their horror after finding one of the murdered officers. They described how Fiona Bone was hit in the head by a bullet at point blank range and was lying dead next to a Taser, which had not been fired. Nicola Hughes was said to have run off to escape the gunman, but had a grenade thrown at her before she was shot. She was found lying in the road pleading for help, and died later in hospital. Post mortems showed that both officers had died of gunshot wounds.

A witness said: "I heard a bang that shook the house so I ran out and saw a woman on the floor who I could tell was already dead – there was blood all over her … I think the younger officer tried to run because she was further away from the house."

Within a very short space of time more than 45,000 messages of support had been received by GMP. Sir Peter said: "We would like to say a huge thank you to the public for this great show of support. I cannot tell you how much it means to us at this most difficult time." A steady stream of people laid floral tributes at the scene of the murders.

On 21st September 2012, heavily armed police stood guard as Cregan appeared in court accused of four murders. Amid unprecedented security, newly bearded Cregan was driven to the hearing in a Ford Transit van in a six-vehicle convoy. In court, he was flanked by five armed officers, while in the well of the court stood two more policemen dressed in military-style fatigues and carrying rifles. Two other armed officers sat in the public gallery. A ring of steel surrounded the court, with at least 20 other officers carrying Heckler & Koch sub-machine guns keeping watch while others could be seen on top of surrounding buildings. Cregan was charged with murdering Fiona and Nicola, and David and Mark Short, as well as four further counts of attempted murder involving three men and a woman. In a dramatic development, it was revealed that a boy of 15 had also been arrested in connection with the four murders. He was released on bail pending further inquiries. Cregan looked gaunt as he scanned the courtroom and stared across at relatives of the Short family during the two-minute hearing, and he spoke only to confirm his name and date of birth as the charges were put to him. Because of the nature of the alleged offences, the case was referred to the city's crown court, where he was to appear the following week. There was no application for bail by his solicitor, David Caplin. The judge, Mr Jonathan Taaffe, told Cregan: "You will be remanded into custody until that time.

Please go with the officers." He was then transferred by armed convoy back to Strangeways jail.

As forensic investigators continued to probe the crime scene where the two police officers died, individuals and groups turned up from all over the Tameside division and wider Greater Manchester force area to stand in silence. Crime investigators, meanwhile, drafted in a fire brigade aerial platform to give them a better vantage point to film and photograph the scene as they continued to build their case. Assistant Chief Constable Garry Shewan said: "This remains a complex and sensitive operation. We ask the public to search their conscience and urge anyone who has any other information to contact us."

On 24th September, the Honorary Recorder of Manchester, Judge Andrew Gilbart, QC, ordered politicians and senior police officers to stop talking about the accused in case it prevented a fair trial. He said: "Deciding what happened ... is a matter for a jury not for the media, police or politicians." He said Sir Peter had spoken "movingly" of the loss of his officers, but added: "The time has come for comment to cease." Meanwhile, Cregan appeared via videolink at Manchester Crown Court and was remanded to appear at Liverpool Crown Court the following month.

At exactly 10.58 on Tuesday 25th September, a week after the two officers were gunned down, more than 500 officers stood shoulder to shoulder with locals and community leaders to remember Fiona Bone and Nicola Hughes. The crowd fell silent to pay their respects. Both women's families were also present.

In October, a teenager who taunted police about the two murdered WPCs, was ordered to build a memorial to them. The 16-year-old boy spouted sick abuse after being arrested for carrying a cosh. He was given a rehabilitation order at Tameside youth court and told to help build a garden dedicated to the two officers in Hattersley.

In early November, Cregan denied murdering Fiona and Nicola when he appeared via videolink during the court hearing. He also denied murdering David and Mark Short and the four further counts of attempted murder. He appeared alongside nine other co-defendants, including eight who faced murder charges linked to the father and son killings. Another defendant stood accused of assisting an offender, Liverpool Crown Court was told. Cregan was remanded in custody to appear at a murder trial at Preston Crown Court in February 2013.

The memorial garden for Fiona and Nicola was opened in December 2012. In a moving ceremony, Paul Bone told those gathered that the garden was "a wonderful, lasting tribute". He continued: "I hope this garden serves as a reminder to the people of Manchester of the work done and the sacrifices made by the police on their behalf."

On 4th February 2013, in the public gallery at Preston Crown Court were Nicola's grieving parents, Susan and Bryn, alongside Fiona's mum and dad, Paul and June, and the WPC's partner Clare Curran. A heavily armed taskforce of 150 officers was in action when Cregan appeared. Police swarmed in and out as the 29-year-old took his seat in the dock charged with killing Fiona and Nicola and the murders of David and Mark Short. Armed officers escorted Cregan and nine other defendants to and from court in prison vans. All 10 men denied the various charges against them – including helping or taking part in one of the four killings, firearms offences or assisting an offender. Three days later, the jury in the trial heard that Cregan was already at the centre of a nationwide manhunt when the WPCs were lured to their deaths: police were on his trail over the killing of David Short and his son.

The prosecution case was outlined by Nicholas Clarke, QC, who said that Cregan ambushed the unarmed officers after reporting a "spurious burglary" at a home in Hattersley, Greater Manchester: "He lay in wait with a Glock firearm with an extended magazine that was fully loaded. Police officers Fiona Bone and Nicola Hughes attended. As soon as they arrived, Cregan shot the officers repeatedly until his magazine was empty. As he left the scene he threw a grenade towards the victims." The jury of seven men and five women also heard that Mark Short was shot dead in a pub on 25th May 2012 and that Cregan was arrested 12 days later. After two days of questioning he was bailed and went on the run.

Two months later, David Short was killed at his home following a bitter family rivalry. Mr Clarke said: "The Short family had been involved in a long-standing feud with members of another local family, the Atkinsons. The families had reached a state of uneasy peace following their lengthy dispute." But the court heard that on 13th May 2012 there was a row between Raymond Young, a member of the Short family, and Theresa Atkinson, described as "the matriarch of the Atkinson family". The bust-up resulted in her allegedly being slapped as she drank at the Cotton Tree pub in Droylsden after she lashed out with a bottle, striking Young. She then threatened Young before contacting her son, Leon, who allegedly cooked up a brutal reprisal for the way his mother had been "disrespected". It was claimed that Leon Atkinson didn't want to "get his hands dirty", so he texted Cregan with instructions to carry out the revenge attack; to shoot dead members of the Short family.

Twelve days after the drunken row the Short family were back in the pub with friends. CCTV footage was shown to the jury of a blue Ford Focus pulling up outside the pub at 11.49pm. The car's hazard lights were switched on before someone got out of the vehicle and ran into the building. Mr Clarke said the killer entered the pub wearing a black balaclava. He added: "The gunman took a single step into the pub and lifted his right arm. In his outstretched hand was a gun. The gun was fired." A volley of seven shots was unleashed, leaving Mark Short dead and three other men injured. The killer fled, jumping into the Ford Focus, which sped off. Mr Short senior, who was also in the pub, held his son in his arms as the young man died.

On 10th August, David Short, also a target as head of the

Short family, was at home in Clayton when he was ambushed. He was shot nine times, and according to prosecutors ballistics tests showed the murder weapon was the same Glock pistol that was used in the killings of the WPCs. Describing Mr Short's death, Mr Clarke said: "He was chased through the house and shot many times. He tried to run around the side of the house to escape. His injuries were already unsurvivable and then a grenade was thrown on to him. Its explosion had devastating consequences for his torso. It was the first time in this country that a military grenade has been deployed in this way."

Minutes after the killing, Sharon Hark was attacked at her home two miles away. The jury heard that Cregan had a grievance with her family. Mr Clarke told Preston Crown Court: "An attempt to shoot her was foiled when the gun misfired. A grenade was thrown at the front of the house. Another grenade was detonated in the back of the hired van being used by the gang. They then escaped in a second vehicle, laid up for the purposes of escape. They then went on the run."

Leon Atkinson (35), Luke James Livesey (27), Damian Gorman (38), Ryan David Hatfield (28) and Matthew Gary James (33) all denied one charge of murder and three of attempted murder. Francis Steven Dixon (37) denied one charge of murder, one of attempted murder and one of causing an explosion. Anthony Wilkinson (33) denied a charge of murder, one of attempted murder, one of causing an explosion and one of possession of a firearm with intent to endanger life. Jermaine Anton Ward (24) denied one charge of murder, one of attempted murder and one of causing an explosion. Mohammed Imran Ali (32) denied assisting an offender. Cregan denied all charges, and the trial continued.

On 8th February 2013 Cregan's movements and the final horrific moments of Fiona and Nicola were described in "chilling detail" to the jury. The night before, it was stated that Cregan had forced his way into the home of a "terrified" family, armed with a Glock pistol, which held 33 bullets. He sent one of the occupants for beer, cigarettes and cigars, and tried to buy cocaine.

CCTV footage from the next morning showed Nicola and Fiona climbing into a police van at Hyde Police station. Nicola was driving. They arrived at the scene at 10.52am. "They were wearing standard issue police body armour. Fiona Bone carried a Taser, but they were otherwise unarmed. Cregan's carefully laid plan had been successful. He had in fact lured two unarmed officers to his door and he was armed, ready and waiting for them. As Nicola and Fiona walked through the small front garden, he opened the front door and immediately fired his Glock. Both officers were shot to the chest. The body armour protected them and the bullets did not penetrate. Examination of the scene after the event shows that after the first shots, both officers made a tactical retreat.

"Fiona Bone moved to her left, getting out of the line of sight, and Nicola Hughes turned to run up the path but as she retreated more shots were fired. Nicola was shot, just below her armoured vest, in the middle of her back, causing her to fall forwards, paralysed on the path. As she was falling or lying flat on her stomach, she was shot three more times. Cregan then turned his attention to Fiona. She was trapped in front of the lounge and he discharged 24 shots at her.

"Some struck the officer, others the house. She managed to draw and fire her Taser, but it was discharged into a hard surface, probably the paving. Such was the speed of the attack upon the two officers that only a matter of 31 seconds had elapsed between Nicola Hughes switching off the engine of their vehicle and Fiona Bone firing the Taser." Mr Clarke added: "Fiona was shot between five and eight times, receiving a total of eight gunshot or related injuries. As she turned and fell one bullet managed to get through under her arm, in a gap in her body armour. She was killed by a perforating shot to the upper side of her chest which caused fatal injuries to the top of her heart.

"Cregan was not finished. He turned his attention back to Nicola, who lay paralysed on the floor, and fired three more shots into the back and side of her head. One ricocheted off the back of her body armour without causing her injury. She was shot eight times, causing a total of seven gunshot related injuries. Four of the shots caused potentially fatal wounds. One had severed her spinal cord, causing instant paralysis and a potentially fatal wound to a major artery. The three final shots fired into the head severely damaged her brain."

Cregan then threw a "fragmentation grenade" at the stricken officers. This exploded, causing further injuries to Nicola, who was nearest the weapon. As traumatized relatives sobbed and clung to each other, the jury heard how at just past 10.00am Cregan made a 999 call, claiming a concrete slab had been thrown through the window of the house. The five-minute call was played to the court, and Cregan was heard reporting the fabricated attack. During the call, he called himself Adam Gartree, and his tone was calm and measured. Mr Clarke said: "The last comment made by the caller was: 'I'll be waiting.'" He then added: "Cregan knew that the officers who attended would have no idea what would be waiting for them."

Cregan then sped away in a BMW to Hyde police station. He went to the front counter, apparently trying to make a call on his mobile phone. PC Snelson immediately recognized the fugitive, who said to him: "I dropped the gun at the scene and I've murdered two police officers. You were hounding my family so I took it out on yours." When it was later suggested he was a coward because he had not waited for armed officers to arrive, he said: "Cos you couldn't fucking find me, could yous." Mr Clarke said Cregan had given himself up to avoid a confrontation with armed police that would probably have led to his own death. He still denied the four murders and causing an explosion.

It transpired that the row in a pub had been sparked by a

"spurned advance". Partner of David Short, Michelle Kelly, told the court: "This woman came up to Dave and flung her arms around him. She was a bit giddy – she'd had a bit to drink. She asked Dave if he wanted a drink but he told her he was out with his missus. She was being disrespectful. I said if I'd not been ill I would have planted her one. She said sorry." Theresa Atkinson then went on to have the row with Raymond Young at another pub, leading to the four murders and four attempted murders.

Three days into the murder trial, Cregan shocked the jury when he admitted luring the two police officers into a trap so that he could gun them down. He sensationally changed his pleas in the afternoon session, when his barrister, Simon Csoka, QC, asked trial judge Mr Justice Holroyde for the two charges to be put to Cregan again. Cregan stood in the dock as the clerk of the court read the charges to him and asked: "How do you now plead?" The killer, who showed no reaction, stood and answered: "Guilty." He had previously said in a police interview: "Sorry about those two that have been killed, I wish it was men." Cregan continued to deny murdering Mr Short and his son. However, he was to remain on trial for their deaths.

The drug dealer Cregan, dubbed the "one-eyed maniac" by newspapers, admitted to a psychiatrist that he had killed the father and son before going on to murder Fiona and Nicola, the court was told on 21st March. He allegedly said he had "the best sleep of my life" after shooting David Short and then throwing the grenade that blew his body apart. Consultant forensic psychiatrist Dr James Collins said that Cregan, who claimed to earn up to £20,000 a week from drugs, admitted all four killings during an interview in jail, and accused David Short of threatening to rape his sister. He allegedly said: "I did feel better after killing him." Cregan added: "I used to think about stabbing him repeatedly, smashing his head with a hammer and cutting his head off." The gangster's confessions in jail about David and Mark Short were the "worst kept secret in Strangeways", the jury heard.

Cregan's barrister, Simon Csoka, QC, said: "When he sets out to kill, he kills. He is going to die in prison." But he told the jury that they should acquit Cregan of attempting to murder Sharon Hark by throwing a hand grenade at her house because the attack was "random". It transpired that with two officers already gunned down in cold blood, "evil" Cregan planned to carry on his murderous mission using a stash of hidden fragmentation grenades. He had secreted 10 of the lethal weapons down a drain ready to blow up any police officers hunting him. But, believing false gangland rumours that he would be killed by armed police as they closed in, he "chickened out" of his deadly plot and handed himself in.

Cregan started his prison sentence, which will keep him in jail until he dies, on 13th June 2013. Relief spread among officers that the grenades had been found – the day before the jury retired to consider its verdict. Officers had feared that the M75 Yugoslavian weapons – which are able to kill within a 45-foot radius and are packed with 3,000 tiny steel balls to create maximum destruction – could have been used by other gangland thugs who were willing to launch more horrific attacks. They were found in Oldham less than 10 miles from the spot where Fiona and Nicola were murdered. The verdict on "brutal" Cregan was welcomed by the WPCs' families, who paid emotional tributes to their loved ones outside court. Paul Bone said he wanted the killer "hanged", and added: "In certain circumstances I think it would be a good idea and this possibly is one of them. My family is still coming to terms with our loss and not a day goes by without thinking of Fiona. I am told it gets easier in time but for the moment every Tuesday lunchtime is difficult, for that was when our lives changed forever." Nicola's mum, Sue, and stepfather, Mike, said of Cregan in a statement: "He has lost nothing. He had already committed two murders and was destined for a lifetime behind bars. He chose, on that day, to murder our daughter and leave our lives devastated, a life barely worth living without her. He will return to his cell to live the rest of his life. We, however, will live with what he did every single hour of every single day for the rest of our lives. Nicola was first and foremost our daughter and sister to her younger brother Sam. Our only daughter – beautiful, loving, thoughtful, caring, hard-working and happy. She embraced everything she did throughout her life with total commitment and enthusiasm. She touched the hearts of everyone she came into contact with and who were part of her life.

"She was planning her future with her boyfriend Gareth and had just become the proud godmother of Jack. She had so much to look forward to, a bright future, one she had worked hard for and one she deserved to live to the full." Nicola's dad, Bryn Hughes, added: "She was brutally and callously murdered in the most despicable and cowardly way. We can only imagine what thoughts and feelings she experienced in those few seconds it took for him to pull the trigger and for Nicola to draw her last breath. Our lives have been shattered. To have a child taken from you in such a cruel and meaningless way is the worst thing any parent can wish to imagine."

Detective Superintendent Simon Barraclough, who led the investigation into the murders, said: "I think he's been relieved that they were both female officers, because in his mind it will have made the job easier. He's an immense coward. His greatest fear would have been if they had been armed. We know he was a coward because he was so keen to get rid of all his weapons before driving to Hyde police station. He was frightened he was going to get shot if there had been a confrontation." Greater Manchester Police Federation chairman Ian Hanson branded Cregan an "abomination upon our society". He added: "He has forfeited his right to walk the streets for the rest of his life. I have no problem with the thought of him staring through one eye at a locked cell door wondering what kind of life he is missing. And after he has stopped being a drain on society he can rot in hell. If anybody thinks that's harsh then I am afraid they are just going to have to live with it."

Mr Justice Holroyde told the convicted man: "You, Cregan, drew those two officers into a calculated trap for the sole purpose of murdering them in cold blood. They survived the first shots and you then pursued them in ruthless determination to end their lives. You shot PC Hughes in the back and left her paralysed before you went back and fired some 20 shots at PC Bone and then returned to PC Hughes to make sure you had killed her by firing further shots at her head. You then exploded a hand grenade over the body of PC Hughes and acted with premeditated savagery."

When Cregan was jailed, along with five members of the gang he recruited to execute David and Mark Short, he smiled and shook hands with the four others in the dock. The killer, from Droylsden, went to jail with a gangland price on his head for murdering his bitter rivals. Their friends vowed to assassinate him. Consultant criminal psychologist Elie Godsi said that he might have killed the two officers because at the time he thought "he wanted to go out in some sort of distorted blaze of glory and gain notoriety for himself". Sir Peter said that the criminals had made themselves out to be "Mr Bigs, glamorizing themselves as some sort of folk heroes who rule through violence, intimidation and reputation". In reality they spent their miserable lives looking over their shoulders to see who was coming after them and their families. He continued: "If the rest of civilization contributed the same as these individuals we would all still be living in caves."

After his conviction, police were on the hunt for the £7 million in "dirty money" that Cregan had made during seven years of drug pushing, and they were keen to explore possible property deals in Thailand, Spain and the Canary Islands. Cregan also bought property in the Droylsden area, including houses and shops, which he rented out. Livesey and Gorman were found guilty of the murder of Mark Short and the attempted murder of three others. They were sentenced to life, with a minimum of 33 years. Wilkinson admitted murdering David Short and possessing a firearm, and was to serve at least 35 years. Ward was also found guilty of Mr Short's murder and got life with a minimum of 33 years. Ali was found guilty of assisting an offender and jailed for seven years. The four other gang members were cleared of murder.

The *Mirror* reported that before Cregan carried out the murders of Fiona and Nicola he was mainly concerned with making sure he looked his best. Having forced his way into Alan Whitwell's home, he forced the terrified barber to give him a haircut and trim his beard, saying: "I want to look good in court." Cregan pushed his way through the front door and placed a grenade on Mr Whitwell's fireplace, saying: "Do what I say and you won't get hurt." Alan Whitwell and Lisa had been preparing for bed when the killer knocked on their front door. Both believed that Cregan, already wanted for murder, would kill them if they didn't do what he said.

It was also reported that an Abbey Gardens resident named only as Dean, cradled Nicola as her life ebbed away. He said: "I could see Nicola and Fiona in the garden. Fiona wasn't moving. Nicola was near the gate and still breathing. I knew she wasn't going to live but all you can say is, 'Everything will be alright.'" Another neighbour handed him a towel to put over her shoulders to keep her warm. Dean stayed with Nicola until the ambulance arrived.

Cregan had built a career as a terrifying gangland thug for hire by the time he killed Fiona and Nicola. The "hard man" wanted his reputation for extreme violence to make him the most feared enforcer in the north. One of his favourite tortures was to "kerb" people who crossed him over money or drugs. He forced them to lie down in the road and place their mouths on the kerb before jumping on their heads. "He is just one of those people, he won't walk away," said one source. He used his ill-gotten gains to travel the world, staying in the lap of luxury, and it was during one of his frequent trips to Thailand that he lost his left eye: it is believed a gangster he tried to rip off in the seedy resort of Pattaya tortured him – gouging his eye out with a knife. The thug returned to the UK with a black onyx false eye, even more intent on raising hell in his home city of Manchester. He had already shown he was prepared to use violence to control his patch.

One of four children, Cregan was described as "an angelic" looking boy. But his upbringing fell apart when his mum Anita and dad Paul split when he was 10. As his older brother, Dean, spent more time with his dad, Cregan grew closer to his mother and sisters. He was quiet at school and at "the bottom of the ability range". He was bullied on the streets but escaped to fields, where he hunted rabbits with air rifles and a hawk. He was obsessed with knives and enjoyed skinning animals. Aged 19, he was a plasterer and roofer who headed to Tenerife to entice holidaymakers to part with their savings in Callao Salvaje. He ripped off elderly couples for cash in a timeshare scam after plying them with booze in local bars. Cregan kicked rivals off his area and was thought to have links with drug dealers. Expat Duncan Rae from Glasgow said: "His behaviour was awful. I felt so sorry for all those people who were scammed out of money. People might have spent their whole lives building up savings, only to be ripped off by scum like him." Cregan was described by another expat as able to handle himself, and it was said that nobody messed with him.

After three years, Cregan returned home and bulked himself up with steroids, selling them along with cocaine and cannabis. He soon became a drug dealer who boasted he could earn £1 million a year. He also operated as a moneylender, whom pals described as "a lunatic" and "an animal".

He was fanatical about his image and loved to be behind the wheel of a Range Rover, BMW or Mercedes – preferably a four-wheel drive – or a fast motorbike. He wanted to be the centre of attention, the man at the bar with the biggest muscles and the most expensive Armani T-shirt. In a restaurant one day, he sent someone a bottle of wine costing £180. He enjoyed five-star holidays and business-class flights, all funded by his £20,000-a-week activities. At one point he had an arsenal of 10 weapons, including a Mac-10 machine gun. As well as trips to Thailand, Cregan took luxury holidays in Antigua and the Dominican Republic and short breaks in Amsterdam. He had drug contacts across Europe, including in Holland, where he bought his weapons. Usually he stayed close to Manchester, keeping an eye on his family in case rivals targeted them in revenge for the violence he meted out. He had a son with girlfriend Georgia Merriman and began his rise through Manchester's criminal hierarchy. He became the enforcer of a known criminal family – a Joey – the hired muscle who was willing to do the dirty work. He "taxed" people in drug deals by providing cocaine worth £40,000 and then arranging balaclava-clad thugs to snatch it back before demanding the money. He was prepared to deal in any drug – from cannabis to heroin – making 200 mobile phone calls a day. He stabbed, battered or ran over anyone who got in his way. People were too terrified to go to the police. He was eager to join the gangland feud against the rival Short family, whose members had bullied him as a child. Before he lured Fiona and Nicola to their deaths, he went on the run in Anglesey, North Wales, Leeds and Herne Bay, Kent. With Cregan in jail, he can no longer protect his own family, who are reported to live in fear for their lives.

As soon as Cregan was jailed for life, vicious threats began to circulate around the underworld. One gang boss put up the £20,000 bounty on Cregan's remaining eye, and he was warned that he was a "dead man walking". On Cregan's Manchester turf, however, those who had helped convict him and his thugs were fleeing their homes as they feared for their safety. Just minutes after he was found guilty, social networking sites were awash with death threats from both sides. Entire communities began to fear that tit-for-tat violence would return to their streets. The Short family grave was vandalized in a hammer attack and tributes were smashed, while reporters spoke to one woman who was prepared to abandon her home because she had given evidence against Cregan at his trial. Cregan, it was reported, hadn't seemed at all bothered that he would die behind bars, and was said to have "laughed like a loon" as he was taken from the court following sentencing.

In July 2013, it was reported that Cregan wanted to be transferred to Ashworth Hospital in Maghull, Merseyside, claiming that his mental health was deteriorating. There were those who were convinced that Cregan just wanted to play the system and to enjoy a more relaxed environment; others thought he was playing a game, but wasn't fooling anyone. By September, though, Cregan had been sent to the same psychiatric unit as Moors murderer Ian Brady, after a month on hunger strike. He was housed in a unit for the criminally insane. Chief Constable Sir Peter Fahy said he didn't care where Cregan was kept as long as he wasn't released. He urged the public to concentrate on Fiona and Nicola's families instead. Cregan was said to have told his family towards the end of 2013 he deserved to die for his murder rampage. At the same time he was said to have expressed his remorse for what he had done. Whether or not that is true, the fact that he said he was sorry and wanted to die early from incurable cancer must hold cold comfort for the families of Fiona and Nicola. Both loved the job they did, both came from loving supportive families who were proud of them, and both were in love and looking forward to their future. It took one deluded, cold-blooded killer just 31 seconds to take it all away, and to cause everlasting devastation.

Jack Huxley

(2013)

A young man knifed to death his step-grandmother after surfing the internet for "granny porn". Jack Huxley (20) armed himself with kitchen knives and a carving fork and stabbed Janis Dundas (62) up to 28 times as she slept. She had given him a bed for the night after he turned up on her doorstep, apparently homeless; she spent most of the day that she was killed trying to find a put-me-up bed for him. Her body was found naked, with evidence that her step-grandson had engaged in "sexual activity" with her. Checks on her computer revealed he had scored it for pornography over a four-hour period leading up to the attack in Ellesmere Port, Cheshire.

On the first day of his trial on 2nd October 2013, at Liverpool Crown Court, Huxley pleaded guilty to murder. His barrister, Charles Miskin, QC, said: "This was a galvanic explosion of violence catalyzed by some sexual component." Huxley was convicted and sentenced to life with a minimum term of 21 years and eight months. He had taken a cocktail of alcohol and drugs at the time of the murder and had been taken in by Mrs Dundas after he had been made an "outcast" by his family, owing to his reliance on drink and drugs. The Recorder of Liverpool, Judge Clement Goldstone, said: "Within less than 24 hours you were to repay that kindness and common decency in a way which was as inhuman as it was gratuitously violent."

On the night of the murder, Huxley did not go to bed. Instead, he searched Mrs Dundas's computer for hardcore pornographic websites – not just any hardcore pornographic websites, but those which were able to satisfy an interest in sexual activity between young men and mature women. Earlier that day, he had carried out the same searches on his own laptop, and also returned to the victim's computer to search for hardcore porn after he had murdered her.

Judge Goldstone said: "I am sure that on that night you spent some considerable time on such websites … in order to arouse yourself sexually with a view to having intercourse with her." The judge said he was "in no doubt whatsoever" that Huxley not only planned to have sex with his step-grandmother, but that he did have penetrative sex with her that night. He added: "I am sure that, in fact, your sexual assault upon her began and continued either whilst she was asleep or not responding." Huxley said one of the reasons he carried out the assault was his apparent inability to form a sexual relationship or any meaningful relations with a girl of his own age. The court heard that after the sexual assault Huxley armed himself with four kitchen knives and the carving fork and went on to mutilate and murder Mrs Dundas. The judge said that only Huxley knew why he had murdered his step-grandmother, but that there could only be two reasons: "Either you were so frustrated by the unsatisfactory sex that had taken place, or you were so disgusted by what you had done that you decided, there and then, to kill her." Huxley launched an attack of "massive ferocity" which continued after Mrs Dundas died, the court heard.

Huxley dragged the pensioner's body off the bed and on to the floor and carried on stabbing her, leaving the four knives sticking out of her back. He also tried to "impale" her foot to the floor. After the murder, Huxley tried to carry out a quick clean up of the flat before again viewing pornography and finally fleeing the scene, stealing the victim's mobile phone, credit card, cash and her car, which he later crashed. He was arrested on suspicion of drink-driving and was found to be under the influence of alcohol, cannabis and other drugs, as well as prescription drugs taken from the victim's home. After his arrest, he tried to "blacken" Mrs Dundas's character by claiming he killed her in self-defence after she tried to sexually assault and attack him. He also claimed he had seen a "masked stranger", before he changed his plea to guilty.

The court heard that Huxley, from Ellesmere Port, Cheshire, had a "difficult and troubled" childhood and that he was "vulnerable to psychotic symptoms" and was clinically depressed and immature. The court also heard that he suffered from neuro-developmental disorder and substance use disorder. Judge Goldstone described Mrs Dundas, a retired mental health nurse, as a "devoted" mother and grandmother, and said her family had been left "devastated" by their loss. After the sentencing, Jessica Knight, the victim's daughter, said: "She was a mummy, a grandmother, sister and daughter, a clever and insightful woman murdered so brutally by a man she had invited into her home. Her murder has left a deep and dark hole in our lives. The sentence imposed in some ways reflects the gravity of this crime and gives us some consolation." She added: "Our wonderful life has been shattered and all we can now do is try not to let the incomprehensible actions of one man become our focus. Instead, we will try to rejoice in the memories we have for a truly wonderful woman, our beautiful mummy."

Detective Inspector Peter Case, of the Cheshire Police Major Investigation Team, who led the investigation, said Huxley's accessing of hardcore pornography was clearly linked to the murder. He said: "At the time of her death, Janis was not in the best of health and was recovering from a hip operation which hindered her mobility. Janis lived in a one bedroom flat, but despite this she agreed to let Jack Huxley sleep in her living room as she wanted to help him. Tragically Janis did not know that Huxley had a fascination with internet porn, particularly ones which involved older women.

"While Janis was in bed Huxley trawled the internet for porn and brutally murdered her while she slept. Huxley then mutilated her after her death. He then washed himself of any traces of blood, got dressed and stole property from her home, including her car. To avoid detection he secured the flat and fled the scene ... However, having travelled a short distance from Janis's home he crashed it and was arrested by police."

Mr Case added: "Evidence suggests that Jack Huxley had a sexual motive for killing Janis … This was a truly shocking case and Jack Huxley has shown no remorse throughout this investigation. The level of violence used to kill Janis and her post-death mutilation has shocked all those involved in this investigation, many of whom have worked on numerous homicide inquiries."

Huxley was described by the *Mirror* as "depraved", and his actions and the crime he committed certainly showed this depravity in its entirety. Even the police and forensic experts on the case were shocked at how "sick" his sexually motivated crime was.

He and the others outlined in this book are surely amongst Britain's most depraved killers.

Britain's Most Depraved Killers